LANCHESTER LIBRARY

D0490878

AN INTRODUCTION TO
FUND MANAGEMENT

The Securities & Investment Institute

Mission Statement:

> *To set standards of professional excellence and integrity for the investment and securities industry, providing qualifications and promoting the highest level of competence to our members, other individuals and firms.*

The Securities and Investment Institute is the UK's leading professional and membership body for practitioners in the securities and investment industry, with more than 16,000 members with an increasing number working outside the UK. It is also the major examining body for the industry, with a full range of qualifications aimed at people entering and working in it. More than 30,000 examinations are taken annually in more than 30 countries.

You can contact us through our website *www.sii.org.uk*

Our membership believes that keeping up to date is central to professional development. We are delighted to endorse the Wiley/SII publishing partnership and recommend this series of books to our members and all those who work in the industry. As part of the SII CPD Scheme, reading relevant financial publications earns members of the Securities & Investment Institute the appropriate number of CPD hours under the Self-Directed learning category. For further information, please visit *www.sii.org.uk/cpdscheme*

Ruth Martin
Managing Director

AN INTRODUCTION TO FUND MANAGEMENT

Third Edition

....

Ray Russell

FCMA, FCIS, MSI, CertPFS, ACoI

JOHN WILEY & SONS, LTD

Copyright © 2006   John Wiley & Sons Ltd, The Atrium, Southern Gate, Chichester,
West Sussex PO19 8SQ, England
Telephone (+44) 1243 779777

Email (for orders and customer service enquiries): cs-books@wiley.co.uk
Visit our Home Page on www.wiley.com

Reprinted with corrections September 2006

All Rights Reserved. No part of this publication may be reproduced, stored in a retrieval
system or transmitted in any form or by any means, electronic, mechanical, photocopying,
recording, scanning or otherwise, except under the terms of the Copyright, Designs and
Patents Act 1988 or under the terms of a licence issued by the Copyright Licensing Agency
Ltd, 90 Tottenham Court Road, London W1T 4LP, UK, without the permission in writing of
the Publisher. Requests to the Publisher should be addressed to the Permissions Department,
John Wiley & Sons Ltd, The Atrium, Southern Gate, Chichester, West Sussex PO19 8SQ,
England, or emailed to permreq@wiley.co.uk, or faxed to (+44) 1243 770620

Designations used by companies to distinguish their products are often claimed as trademarks.
All brand names and product names used in this book are trade names, trademarks or registered
trademarks of their respective owners. The Publisher is not associated with any product or
vendor mentioned in this book.

This publication is designed to provide accurate and authoritative information in regard to
the subject matter covered. It is sold on the understanding that the Publisher is not engaged
in rendering professional services. If professional advice or other expert assistance is
required, the services of a competent professional should be sought.

Other Wiley Editorial Offices

John Wiley & Sons, Inc., 111 River Street, Hoboken, NJ 07030, USA

Jossey-Bass, 989 Market Street, San Francisco, CA 94103-1741, USA

Wiley-VCH Verlag GmbH, Boschstr. 12, D-69469 Weinheim, Germany

John Wiley & Sons Australia Ltd, 42 McDougall Street, Milton, Queensland 4064, Australia

John Wiley & Sons (Asia) Pte Ltd, 2 Clementi Loop #02-01, Jin Xing Distripark, Singapore 129809

John Wiley & Sons Canada Ltd, 22 Worcester Road, Etobicoke, Ontario, Canada M9W 1L1

Wiley also publishes its books in a variety of electronic formats. Some content that appears
in print may not be available in electronic books.

Coventry University Library

British Library Cataloguing in Publication Data

A catalogue record for this book is available from the British Library

ISBN-13 978-0-470-01770-8 (PB)
ISBN-10 0-470-01770-8 (PB)

Project management by Originator, Gt Yarmouth, Norfolk (typeset in 12/16pt Trump Mediaeval).
Printed and bound in Great Britain by T.J. International Ltd, Padstow, Cornwall.
This book is printed on acid-free paper responsibly manufactured from sustainable forestry
in which at least two trees are planted for each one used for paper production.

PREFACE

· ·

This guide is derived from the author's notes for the 2-day course of the same name that he presented for the Securities and Investment Institute.

It is neither a transcript of the course, nor a fully comprehensive work of reference. Rather, it is intended as an introductory text for those new to or unfamiliar with investments and asset management by providing a broad and practical description of investment funds and fund management from a number of perspectives and to stimulate further, more detailed study.

Starting with the general economic background and rationale for the existence of funds, it moves through a description of the features and characteristics of different types of funds, and the associated regulatory and investor protection mechanisms, to the process of establishing a fund.

It then addresses the topic from the perspective of the portfolio manager, by providing an overview of the principal investment strategies and styles deployed in the construction of portfolios, and of their administration, before covering investor administration and, finally, the mathematics and methods of performance measurement.

Your own understanding of fund management after reading this guide will depend upon your interest and aspirations, your appetite for and approach to learning, and, of course, your expectations of the guide, which, please note, is an introduction to the subject; it will not make you an expert!

ABOUT THE AUTHOR

Ray Russell FCMA, FCIS, MSI, CertPFS, ACoI is the Principal of GCR Management Services, a consultancy and training organisation he founded in 1988 to provide assistance to investment businesses.

His background includes 10 years as Compliance & Business Development Director of a UK fund management and administration group of companies, and more than 20 years in senior positions with prominent British and American investment banks.

An industry figure, he has served as a consultant to the Securities and Investment Institute for its investment administration qualifications, and on the Investment Management Association's Executive, Regulations, Audit and Training Committees, and is the founder and chairman of its collective investment schemes working practices Technical Discussion Group.

Chapter

1

INTRODUCTION

Fund management is, self-evidently, about managing funds.

We tend to use the word *funds* rather loosely. It can refer to our own hard-earned cash, whether in our pockets or held at a bank, or to the equally hard cash that constitutes the initial amount of capital we have available for investment, as well as to the *vehicles* or medium through which our resulting investments are made and managed.

Thus, you have *personal funds*, comprising the pound in your pocket and the balances you have in your bank or building society account, some of which is likely to be *committed funds*, needed to cover current expenditure, and some of which may not be required for some time, but, nonetheless, is earmarked for a future event. If there's any surplus beyond these two types of commitment, apart from being among the fortunate few, you have *spare funds*.

What you choose to do with your spare funds – and, indeed, with the funds that are not required until some time in the future – is a personal matter. You may regard spare funds as 'fun money' and opt to spend it on whatever takes your fancy. You may take a more responsible attitude to funds set aside or building up to meet future commitments or ambitions, but equally well, may feel you can afford to place at least some of it into an 'investment', as distinct from leaving it to the potential ravages of inflation as 'savings'.

This is where the second use of the word *funds* comes in.

Most individuals lack substantial wealth or enough wealth to make the investment of their personal funds directly into stocks, shares and other investment assets a practical and low-risk endeavour. Equally, most people lack the professional expertise and knowledge of business, markets and individual companies to identify the sheep from the goats, as it were. Then, of course, there's the time and the paperwork associated with keeping track of a personal portfolio and with keeping an eye on your taxation opportunities and obligations – especially onerous under self-assessment.

The advantages and commercial benefits of pooling the modest savings or spare money of a large number of individuals have long been manifest in the form of 'funds' managed centrally by organisations which can provide all the investment and administrative services you could wish for. In its simplest sense, 'fund' could be the Christmas Club or Tontine run from your local club, pub or investment club, but, for the purposes of this guide, we are talking about broader based offerings from institutions such as banks, life companies, pension funds, unit trust managers, stockbrokers and specialist investment houses.

ECONOMIC BACKGROUND

This section is about the money we can think of as *capital* and about investments and investors. Capital is essentially an accounting term that distinguishes the primary amount of money committed to investment from the income that arises from its investment or other deployment.

'Money makes the world go round'

Money is the oil for the wheels of economic activity and, like any commodity, there are those among us who need more than we can generate from our own resources and, fortunately, those who have a surplus to their own requirements.

These are for our purposes the users and the suppliers of capital. In economic terms, users require capital to finance production, whether of goods or services – i.e., to pay for the acquisition and deployment of resources, which can be raw materials, physical plant and equipment or labour or, as they are known today, human resources.

The amount of money required obviously depends upon a number of factors – the scale of the endeavour, the cost of the various resources, how long before the goods or services are ready to be sold, what further costs are involved in preparing them for market, delivering them to customers, after-sales service and so on.

The amount will also vary according to where the user is in the life of the endeavour. The amount required to establish a business and to finance initial production – known as start-up capital – may be considerable.

Similarly, the amount required to maintain production, sales and administration once the business has been established – known as working capital – may be significantly beyond the immediate resources of the business owner. It is only when the revenues from sales come on stream that the business begins to generate cash and the owners can experience a reduction in the need for externally provided capital.

'Money doesn't grow on trees'

Having established that his own funds are insufficient for the enterprise in contemplation, the user of capital needs to find suppliers of capital.

If the amount required is modest, it may well be within the compass of family and friends, but more likely the user will need to look further afield to institutional lenders or investors or, if the business qualifies, to government agencies for grants.

Almost immediately, the user will have to confront issues of control, risk and reward, as the type and terms of lenders' or investors' capital are negotiated. Not all avenues will be open to all users, because not only is the actual amount required a factor, but so are the status of the user in terms of reputation, creditworthiness and business skills, the anticipated length of time the money is required, whether security is required or available, and, similarly, whether an involvement in the running of the business and/or a share in the expected future profits are required or offered, and, of course, the extent to which the user wants to limit liability for the debts of his enterprise.

Risks and rewards

Matching users with suppliers is largely a function of the respective parties' appetite for and attitude towards risk, and their desires and expectations for reward, either to be received as a supplier or given up as a user.

Again assuming some basic knowledge of the structure of limited liability companies, there are different forms that the supply of capital can take and different considerations which apply to the selection of each particular form.

Equity capital

Equity capital denotes the supplier has an ownership interest in the business that is using the capital, and shares in the risks and the rewards associated with operation of the business. If the business is adjudged to represent a sound and profitable venture, the user should have little difficulty finding suppliers of equity. On the other hand, the user will not want to give up more profit or control than is absolutely necessary.

Of interest, possibly, is that the members of William Shakespeare's company – essentially a co-operative – were known as *sharers* and that today's actors' trade union is called *Equity*.

Ordinary shares

Ordinary shares are the most common form of equity capital. Indeed, in the USA and elsewhere, such shares are known as common shares. They provide the permanent capital of the business. The holders have no rights to repayment from the company except upon it being wound up, and then only if there are enough assets to provide a surplus after all debts and preferential creditors have been repaid. As the bearers of the greatest risk, however, ordinary shareholders are entitled to the entire surplus earnings and assets of a business once all other claims have been fulfilled. The higher the risk, the higher the ordinary shareholder expects his reward, either in the form of dividends from distributed profits or from capital growth in the value of his investment from re-invested profits or expectations of future profits.

Preference shares

Preference shares are another form of equity capital and, as the name suggests, the supplier has some preference over ordinary shareholders. Usually, this has to do with the payment and the rate of dividend, which is payable before any dividend can be paid to ordinary shareholders, and, in the event of a winding-up, preference in the allocation of assets or the proceeds from their sale. The suppliers of preference share capital are taking some of the risks associated with ownership – there may be insufficient proceeds from a liquidation to pay them out, either in full or at all, and, particularly in the early years, profits may either not be earned or not earned in sufficient amount to pay the expected dividend. However, the risks are somewhat lower than those of the ordinary shareholder.

Loan or debt capital

Loans and loan stocks are the form of capital favoured by suppliers who want to take minimal risk and seek neither the privileges nor the pitfalls of ownership. The reward for such suppliers is interest, which for the user is a charge on earnings rather than a share of profit, and, on agreed terms, repayment in full. The simplest form is the bank loan, but businesses can raise loan or debt capital by the issue of debenture stock, the terms of which can include fixed or variable interest, phased repayment, unsecured or secured on assets of the business or by guarantee, and rights to convert the stock into equity capital at predetermined future times and on predetermined terms.

When speaking of *debt capital*, we are, of course, referring to the funds raised by companies engaged in some productive activity and supplied in the form of a repayable debt instrument, quite often styled a *corporate bond*. Note also that governments are major issuers of debt instruments to raise capital for a variety of purposes – *government bonds* or *gilts*, so-called because the original certificates provided to lenders were edged in gold leaf, hence *gilt-edged securities*.

Money-market instruments

Though not a form of capital, it is worth mentioning that both users and suppliers make use of the money market when surplus capital needs to be deployed for the short term and with little or no risk of loss. Instruments available include Certificates of Deposit (*CDs*) issued by banks, Commercial Paper *(CP)* issued by major companies, and Treasury Bills issued by the government.

Considerations

Users and suppliers both need to consider the same factors from their different perspectives. For how long is the money required – short term, long term, permanently? What incentives are offered/required to attract the individual types of capital? What is the business climate, both generally and for the business in question? What is the market for the goods or services and what is market sentiment? Fashion? Politics?

All of these factors will affect the demand for and the supply and the price of each type of capital.

At certain times the fashion may be for the supply of equity capital; at others, suppliers may be comparatively risk-averse and prefer loan capital, particularly if the business is speculative or the user an unknown or untried individual or group of people. Consider how users and suppliers would confront the imaginary companies, *Solid Surething plc* and *Dodgy Dot Com Ltd.*

Whatever the reason, money, and hence capital, is a commodity and its price will be set to reflect supply, demand, risks and their ratings, users and their reputation and credit ratings, availability of security or collateral, and, possibly most importantly, the likelihood of and ease of achieving repayment or realisation. Other factors include, for equity capital, any discount or premium in relation to underlying net asset value (actual or perceived) and any 'perks' on offer, and, for debt capital, prevailing market interest rates. In both cases, the conceptual appeal of the enterprise will also have a bearing – Eurotunnel, for example.

Markets

If the business is a large enterprise, then the instruments representing ownership or supply of the various forms of capital will probably themselves be capable of assignment or transfer to another person, and we have, thereby, the concept of transferable securities and the opportunity for a market in the investments themselves.

Short-term funding usually takes the form of bank lending and banks themselves operate a money market on which supply and demand can be balanced and prices – i.e., interest rates – set accordingly, based upon prevailing and expected future conditions, the status of the borrower and the time period for which money is required, which can be as short as overnight or as long as a year or two. The amounts can be very big and sometimes too big for one bank to supply, in which case a syndicate of lending banks may be organised by the 'lead bank' to raise the required loan.

The term *money market* is applied to sterling-denominated instruments, and a variation on the money market is the foreign exchange market, which facilitates both the financing of trade denominated in foreign currencies and the trading of the currencies and currency instruments themselves.

Medium- to long-term funding is likely to take the form of equity capital or loan stock, both of which can be traded on a stock exchange.

Markets perform two important and related functions. As a recognised forum for the purpose of matching users and suppliers of capital, a market can operate both as a primary market, wherein the initial or new capital is raised, and as a secondary market, wherein the suppliers of capital may trade amongst themselves and transfer ownership of the various types of capital raised by the user.

Investment instruments

'Instrument' is simply the generic name given to documents evidencing ownership or supply of the various forms of capital. Increasingly in a dematerialised world, where such evidence is purely a record held in electronic form, 'instrument' has come to mean also the form of capital itself.

'Neither a borrower nor a lender be'

Economic activity, the wealth of a community and the rate of growth in both depends, on the one hand, on the existence of innovators, producers and entrepreneurs, generally, and, on the other, their backers or people willing to put at risk their own funds to support the activity. So, the captioned admonition is misguided except in the limited context of managing one's own affairs or funds prudently!

Investors are crucial to the health, wealth and growth of an economy and the profile of an investor is what summarises his or her objectives, attitude toward risk and liquidity, and the timescale over which those objectives and attitudes apply.

The most important decisions a supplier of capital has to make are the extent to which he wants to share the business risks, and, if this is 'not at all', the terms on which he is happy to lend.

Chapter

2

....

ROLE OF FUNDS

Definitions

I refer you back to the introduction for the definition of 'funds', which for our purpose is the mechanism whereby the contributions of many individuals are pooled and managed as a single fund.

Management of the fund is usually taken to refer to the investment management – i.e., the buying and selling of the investments comprising the fund's portfolio, but the fund manager actually takes responsibility for a wide range of activities, and is organised as a business itself, with specialist departments to deal with each of the activities.

The manager is, in effect, facilitating intermediation between the users of capital and the suppliers, typically but not necessarily small suppliers. This is achieved, depending on the purpose of the fund, by being a provider of new capital in the primary market – e.g., a venture capital trust, and/or by providing liquidity in the secondary market as a buyer and seller of investments.

'Fund management' companies are usually organised into front-, mid- and back-offices which deal with the various aspects of the business – namely, marketing, portfolio management, transaction processing, systems support, fund accounting and administration, compliance and corporate management.

Investment businesses

Most funds are themselves investments and, therefore, fund management is a 'designated investment business' and a 'regulated activity'.[1] These terms have specific meanings attaching to them by virtue of the Financial Services and Markets Act 2000, which is the primary legislation governing the conduct of investment business in the UK. Schedule 2 Part II lists the instruments constituting 'investments' and Part I lists the activities involving investments that constitute 'regulated activities'. Excluding 'deposit taking' and certain insurance and mortgage businesses the latter corresponds to 'designated investment business'.

Importantly for pooled funds, Part XVII provides the legislation governing the establishment and operation of 'collective investment schemes', which is the generic term used by regulators for pooled funds organised as unit trusts or investment companies.

So, who's in investment business? Again, as heralded in the introduction, the answer includes banks, brokers, life insurers, pension scheme managers, investment houses, unit trust managers and trustees and, comparatively recently brought within the definition, nominee companies and custodians.

---

[1] The Regulated Activities Order is a Statutory Instrument that is varied from time to time.

Types of fund

The types of fund are closely allied to their purpose, which can sometimes be deduced from their names.

Life funds

A 'life fund' is a pool of money contributed to a life assurance company and invested for the purpose of providing benefits upon death or the expiry of a certain period of time. Legal ownership of the investments acquired by the life fund vests with the life company, which has contracts with the ultimate beneficiaries, known as policies. Payment of benefits is determined by the terms of each policy and, whilst the value of with-profits (as distinct from fixed or guaranteed) benefits is significantly influenced by the value of the life fund and its performance over the life of the contract, a number of other factors may be influential in the actuary's determination.

Pension funds

A 'pension fund' is a pool of money contributed to a pension scheme and invested to provide either an actual pension to participants when they retire (*defined benefit scheme*) or a sum of money that is used to buy an annuity (*defined contribution* or *money purchase scheme*). The scheme may also provide for death in service benefits and widows' pensions and is, therefore, frequently linked to a life policy or provided by a life company. Broadly, with a defined benefits or final salary scheme, which used to be the only form of pension scheme available to employees, contributions are made by the employer but, from the employee's perspective, the scheme may be contributory or non-contributory. With a money purchase scheme, contributions are invested to grow into a pot of money which is realised at a future date and used to purchase a stream of income known as an 'annuity'. Pension schemes today may be provided by employers or be set up as personal pensions by individuals. Recent legislation has updated the requirements of pension fund trustees and established The Pensions Regulator (*TPR*) as a regulatory body separate from the Financial Services Authority (*FSA*).

Unit trusts

'Unit trusts' are the most common form of collective investment scheme in the UK and are legally constituted as a trust with the purpose of providing income and/or capital growth from a portfolio of investments acquired with the pool of funds contributed by the unit-holders. The trustee is the legal owner of the investments but he must deal with the investments in the manner instructed by the manager and ensure that the scheme's capital and income are applied in the best interests of the beneficial owners, who are the unit-holders. The price of units is determined according to regulations and based upon the value of the underlying assets, including income of the trust, plus or minus permitted charges.

Common Investment Funds

A 'Common Investment Fund' (*CIF*) is a special form of collective investment scheme that can be established as a trust and as a charity under the Charities Act. Investment in CIFs is restricted to charities registered in England and Wales (or recognised by HM Revenue and Customs as such a charity) only.

Investment trusts

'Investment trusts' are not trusts but limited liability companies which have shareholders, whose funds are invested in the shares of other companies for the same purposes as unit trusts. Instead of a trustee, investment trusts have a custodian as the registered holder of the fund's investments and, instead of a manager, a board of directors to manage the company. Investment management and administration are usually sub-contracted to a specialist fund management company. The shares of investment trusts are themselves traded on the stock exchange. The price of such shares is, therefore, a function of supply and demand in the stock market and may be at a premium or discount to the underlying asset value per share.

Open-Ended Investment Companies (OEICs)

Open-Ended Investment Companies (*OEICs*) or Investment Companies with Variable Capital (*ICVCs*) are the newest form of collective investment scheme permitted in the UK, combining features of both unit trusts and investment trusts. They are companies with variable capital, established originally under special legislation drawn up under the European Communities Act 1972 but now under the Financial Services & Markets Act and the Open-Ended Investment Companies Regulations 2001 issued by the FSA. Although with some features that are common to all companies, OEICs are not governed by the Companies Acts. Like an investment trust, an OEIC can be managed by its board of directors, one of whom must be the Authorised Corporate Director (*ACD*) taking responsibility for principal operating matters. The ACD can be the sole director, making it the equivalent of the manager of the unit trust. Assets are held by a depositary, who also has some responsibilities of oversight of the ACD, shares of different classes can be issued and they are 'single-priced' based on the mid-market values of the company or, in the case of an umbrella company, the relevant subfund's Net Asset Value (*NAV*). The shares may be listed but are more likely to be bought and sold through the ACD, who is permitted to add or deduct charges like a unit trust manager and to apply a 'dilution levy' on behalf of the fund if mid-pricing would distort unfairly the NAV per share relationship between shareholders on the issue or redemption of a large number of shares.

Private portfolios

'Private portfolios' are simply a collection of investments under single ownership, whether an individual, club, charity, company or other organisation and managed as a *segregated fund*. No special rules apply. The owner is free to invest how he chooses, although some private portfolios arise under wills or similar private trusts, when the trustee is constrained by the terms of the trust. Although such funds are not open to public investment, they can be a significant source of capital for new ventures or ventures seeking to raise fresh capital.

Offshore funds

An 'offshore fund' should not be thought of as a high-risk, high-cost way of hiding investment assets from the UK authorities in a foreign tax haven, but simply as a collective investment scheme established outside of the UK, usually in the form of an open-ended company and issuing shares on a similar basis to the UK OEIC. Schemes established in the EU that are Undertakings for Collective Investment in Transferable Securities (*UCITS*) are eligible to be marketed in the UK subject to recognition by the FSA and compliance with UK marketing rules. The most dominant forms for funds established in Europe (outside Ireland, which adopts the term *UCITS Funds*) are those established in France and Luxembourg as Société d'Investissement à Capital Fixe (*SICAF*) or Organismes de Placement Collectif en Valeurs Mobilières (*OPCVMs*) which can be either:

- Société d'Investissement à Capital Variable (*SICAV*), or
- Fond Commun de Placement (*FCP*).

Similar funds established in 'designated territories' – i.e., those with close links to the UK, such as the Channel

Islands, Isle of Man and Bahamas, may also be recognised by the FSA.

Venture Capital Trusts

'Venture Capital Trusts' (*VCT*) are companies similar to investment trusts but with tax concessions for investors provided that within 3 years from its launch the company has invested at least 70% of its assets in new issues of smaller unquoted (or AIM-listed) companies. There are restrictions on the size of individual investments made each year and on the gross assets of the investee company, which must be carrying out a 'qualifying trade'. The aim is to provide a tax-efficient way for investors to provide capital to non-financial enterprises. Investment in property companies is also restricted. Unlike any but the pension funds described above, the VCT investor may claim tax relief on the amount he invests – at the lower rate on investments of up to £100,000 for any tax year – and is not liable to tax on dividends received (not that much in the way of dividend should be expected from such investments). There are also reliefs from capital gains tax, including deferral of prior gains on investments realised to provide funds for investment in the VCT.

Hedge funds and other

Individual funds may be further classified according to their:

- *asset orientation* – e.g., as stock or equity funds, bond funds, securities funds, money funds, futures and options funds, property or real estate funds or mixed or hybrid funds;

- *investment objective* – e.g., growth funds, income funds, balanced funds and, for funds that seek to emulate the performance of an index, index or tracker funds.

'Hedge funds' constitute a further variation. Although they may properly be classified as 'growth funds', unlike other funds, which are typically 'long-only' funds, they deploy a variety of strategies, including short-selling and derivative positioning across a range of asset classes, in an attempt to make profits in both a rising and a falling market. Many hedge funds do not, in fact, employ hedging techniques and are more accurately described as 'absolute return funds' or 'alternative investment funds', the latter because they invest across the spectrum of asset classes – e.g., combining stocks and shares with commodities and property.

Still further differentiations can be found in structures where one fund invests exclusively in another (master fund and feeder fund), in a number of other funds (fund of funds) or has itself a number of sub-funds (umbrella fund).

A final distinction between funds arises due to their legal structure. Funds may be constituted as companies, as trusts or as partnerships, or they may have a joint ownership structure but no legal personality (such as the French FCP).

Open-ended and closed-ended funds

These descriptors indicate whether a fund is permitted to issue and redeem shares or units on a continuous basis, thereby allowing new investors to enter and existing investors to leave the fund without restriction, or, in either case, to increase or reduce their existing holding. Funds that provide such a facility are 'open-ended' and may fluctuate in size; funds that do not are 'closed-ended' and operate with a fixed amount of capital from the initial launch or subsequent new issues.

Unit trusts and OEICs are examples of open-ended funds; investment trusts and venture capital trusts are examples of closed-ended funds. Investors in the former come and go via dealing with the manager or ACD, whereas investors in the latter are restricted to trading their shares on the stockmarket.

Closed-ended funds retain one at least of the characteristics of the earliest form of collective investment via a trust, the 'fixed trust', which was established with a fixed amount of capital for a fixed period, a fixed portfolio and with a fixed number of participants. None of these features could be varied. Dating from the mid-19th century, many fixed trusts, which in any event were unpopular when investments failed, converted to companies when the legality of investing via a trust was challenged, so creating our present-day investment trust.

The restriction of being closed-ended remained, however; so, in 1931 we imported the idea of a 'flexible trust' from the USA and this is the unit trust as we know it today.

The principal advantages of closed-ended funds accrue to the investment manager, insofar as the portfolio does not have to be adjusted to cope with money coming in or going out. From the investor's point of view, the influence of supply and demand on the price of shares can produce buying opportunities when the price is at a discount to NAV, but since shares usually are at a discount the ultimate value from the investment may not be obtainable unless the fund has a fixed life, and not until its assets are realised and distributed at a predetermined date that marks the end of its life.

The advantages of open-ended funds accrue mainly to the investor. Shares or units are always redeemable at NAV via the manager or equivalent and, as 'regulated products', such funds are covered under the Financial Services Compensation Scheme.

Disadvantages depend on your viewpoint and attitude to risk. Restrictions on the investment powers of unit trusts and OEICs, for example, prevent concentration and provide a diversified portfolio, but also limit the gain that is possible on any single successful investment.

Uses of funds

Funds can be used by investors for two principal purposes – to accumulate capital to deal with some future event, such as mortgage repayment, retirement, school fees, major expenditure; or to provide a current income, whether as a pension, purchase of an annuity or simply supplementary to other sources.

From a user's perspective, funds can be used as a source of capital, as discussed earlier, whether for start-up, expansion or the replacement of plant and machinery.

Associated packaging

Funds are often 'packaged' within a 'wrapper' or a plan, designed to appeal to the particular needs of investors or in response to government initiatives to stimulate investment with tax concessions.

Examples are pension plans, Personal Equity Plans (*PEPs*), school fee plans, savings plans, mortgage repayment plans, Individual Savings Accounts (*ISAs*) and Child Trust Funds (*CTFs*).

The term 'packaged product' is applied by regulators to the fund itself when it is a unit trust or life policy.

FEATURES AND CHARACTERISTICS
Purpose, providers and players

The essential purpose of funds is to make the advantages of pooling available to investors and to users of capital. Bigger pots are available for bigger projects, such as the funding of aircraft or property purchases. More people can take part in and provide a stream of funds for new investment, and whether via a manager or a market, both sides have liquidity facilities. By their variety, funds are a valuable mechanism for balancing risk and reward and matching the needs of users and suppliers of capital.

Given the costs and complexities of operating a large fund for a large number of participants, and the need for the utmost financial strength and probity, the main providers are themselves large organisations, principally insurance companies and banks, or their associated investment subsidiaries. Smaller funds are run by stock-brokers and specialist investment houses.

If the fund is constituted as a trust, the main players are the manager and the trustee, who are the parties to the deed that establishes the fund as a trust. The manager is responsible for all the investment, marketing and normal operational aspects, and the trustee is respons-ible for safeguarding the investments, collecting and distributing income and generally looking out for the interests of holders. Responsibility for maintaining the register of holders rests with either the manager or the trustee, according to the terms of the deed, which, in turn, depends on when the trust was established.

Funds constituted as companies are operated by their board of directors, with the assets held by a custodian or depositary, who ordinarily has similar but fewer responsibilities than a trustee.

In each case, the principal players may delegate functions (but not responsibilities) to other parties specialising in investment management, administration, registration and safe-custody.

Similarly, each type of fund will appoint auditors and/or reporting accountants.

Costs, benefits and comparisons

Some of the costs and benefits associated with funds are discernible from the descriptions of purpose and structure already given but the following will complete the picture:

Costs – to the manager

- Set-up – the formation costs of establishing and obtaining authorisations for itself and for its funds.
- Portfolio management – the costs of hiring and rewarding skilled personnel and installing information and decision support systems.
- Marketing – promoting its services and products to its target investors.
- Administration – establishing adequate staffing, systems and procedures to process its business.
- Communications – installing and maintaining systems and procedures to ensure prompt and effective communications with suppliers, investors and regulators.
- Compliance – all the above must be carried out in a way that delivers regulatory compliance on a

continuing basis, which includes having compliance monitoring staff and documented procedures – failure to comply may result in an unwelcome additional cost in the form of an FSA fine!!

Costs – to the investor

- Initial charge – an amount or percentage added to the cost of purchasing units, or, under dual-pricing, included in the purchase price. The rate varies according to the type of fund, from around 5% for equity growth funds and 2% for international bond funds to less than 1% and sometimes 0% for index funds. This charge is sometimes referred to as a 'front-end', 'preliminary' or 'sales' charge. Funds that make no such charge are often described as 'no-load funds'.
- Exit charge – an amount or percentage that may be deducted from the proceeds of a sale of units. Sometimes described as a 'back-end' or redemption charge, it can be levied only if the manager has described its possible application in its promotional material and only if, when added to any initial charge, it does not exceed the maximum rate allowed for that charge. Exit charges are favoured by managers seeking to attract and retain investors by an initial charge of 0% and a scale of exit charge rates that reduce the longer the units are held, often to 0% after 5 years.
- Annual charge – an amount or percentage of NAV deducted by the manager from the fund's income or, under certain circumstances, its capital. Over time, this is the most significant charge that is borne by investors, albeit one that is suffered only indirectly.

Benefits – to the investor

- Spread of risk – a typical fund will hold a large number of underlying investments, larger than most individuals could afford to hold on their own account, and, thereby, reducing the risk of loss attaching to any one holding.
- Diversification – by spreading the fund's portfolio across asset classes and economic and geographic sectors, the risk of loss is further reduced to the factors that affect all markets.
- Dealing efficiency – fund managers are able to effect transactions to buy or sell a fund's underlying holdings on terms that are significantly better than could be achieved by an individual.
- Tax deferral – funds, typically, are not taxed on their capital gains, thereby allowing unitholders' investments to grow in value faster than if held outside the fund. Any liability to tax is levied on the investor when he sells his holding of units or shares in the fund at a profit.
- Reduced paperwork and administration – the extent and complexity of record-keeping associated with a portfolio of possibly 100 investments can be eliminated by having a single investment in a fund with the same portfolio.
- Professional management – it is the business of fund managers to maintain a continuous watch over the investments held in their funds and to have in place secure and competent custody and administrative arrangements that protect investors' interests.

Benefits to the manager are self-evident: fund management is a business which, operated successfully, can produce significant earnings from the billions entrusted to the care of fund management companies. The greater the fund managers' success in protecting and growing investors' wealth, the more money people will entrust to them and the more they will earn.

Comparisons

Comparisons between the sums invested in different types of fund show the dominance of life and pension funds, notwithstanding the recent trend for faster growth in the sales of unit trusts and OEICs, principally via PEP and ISA investment.

The usual performance comparisons made by fund managers contrast the cumulative result of fund investment versus a building society deposit account. The Investment Management Association (IMA)'s guide for investors claims, for example, that in the 15 years from 1988 to 2003, £1,000 invested in a typical UK All Companies Fund had grown in value to more than £3,400 versus a little over £1,600 for the equivalent building society deposit. Comparisons made prior to this period were even more compelling – a fund investment in 1981 was worth about five times the equivalent building society deposit by 2001. The stockmarket has shown some recovery since 2003 while interest rates have remained low, so the comparison today for a 15–20-year period probably shows that fund growth has outperformed deposit growth some three to four times.

The reason for this is the risk/reward ratio – over the longer term, diversified equity investment will produce higher rewards than deposit-based savings, which carry limited risk and return only interest. Also important is the compounding effect. The successful fund manager will produce capital profits to enlarge the fund and, thereby, increase its earning power and opportunity for further growth. The deposit account capital remains unchanged throughout the life of the account other than the addition of interest. It is only in sustained periods of very high interest rates that better overall returns are achieved by savings vehicles.

How to invest

Much depends on the type of fund involved and the status of the investor. Generally, investment can be divided into lump sum and regular contribution, and the method similarly into single payment by cheque and regular payments by salary deduction, collection by representatives, standing order or direct debit. At least, an initial application form or proposal has to be completed. Subsequent additions or redemptions for funds organised as collective investment schemes may be possible by telephoning instructions to the operator.

Sales, marketing and disclosure

Unless a fund is purely a mechanism for a known group of investors to achieve a specific objective, some form of marketing is needed to attract investors and achieve

sales. Promotion can be via mailshots, press advertisements, other media (TV, radio, Internet) and seminars.
Fund managers may also employ direct sales forces and/
or relationships with independent intermediaries with
access to investors' funds and offer special incentives
by way of discounts or enhanced allocations of units.

With this sort of 'pressure' being applied to the sup-
posedly innocent investor, government is always anxious
to minimise the likelihood of fraud or deception. Consequently, there is considerable legislation and regulation governing how funds may be promoted, including
what must be disclosed to investors prior to making the
investment and subsequently. Under conditions of being
'sold' a packaged product by a sales representative,
investors must be given the right to cancel their instructions or to have a 'cooling-off period' during which they
may change their mind. This is particularly the case for
'distance contracts' – investments made other than by
way of face-to-face interactive dialogues.

Categories, sectors and statistics

From the investor's viewpoint, it is helpful to group
available funds into categories for purposes both of selection and of comparison with like funds. Taking unit
trusts and OEICs as our example, the trade association
(IMA) defines some 30 performance categories, most of
which are based on investment objectives and geographic scope, with some categories reserved for specialist types of fund.

Data that show the overall return achieved from investing in each fund within each category over various
periods are published regularly, typically showing the
current realisable value of £1,000 invested at various
points in the past.

Regulators have another interest in categorising funds,
which is to provide identification by type of fund for
purposes of controlling their investment powers. For
unit trusts and OEICs, the FSA now refers to funds as
being 'UCITS' or 'non-UCITS' schemes, with further
classifications as 'retail', 'non-retail' and 'qualified
investor' schemes, for each of which the FSA has different rules regarding permitted investments. Older funds
may still be governed by FSA rules that define nine
different types of fund, according to investment policy
and ranging from the usual 'securities fund' through
'funds of funds' to the more specialised 'property
funds' and 'futures and options funds'.

INVESTOR PROTECTION

'Be it enacted by the Queen's most Excellent Majesty ...'

These words are conventional text for Acts of Parliament and so begins our primary current piece of investor
protection legislation, the Financial Services & Markets
Act 2000 (FSMA), 'an Act to make provision about the
regulation of financial services and markets; to provide
for the transfer of certain statutory functions relating
to building societies, friendly societies, industrial and

provident societies and certain other mutual societies; and for connected purposes.'

The FSMA creates a new comprehensive legal framework for the provision of financial services in and from the UK, the protection of consumers and the maintenance of orderly markets. It abolishes the old self-regulatory framework established under its immediate predecessor legislation, the Financial Services Act 1986 and the Self-Regulating Organisations (*SROs*) spawned by that Act. It consolidates responsibilities held previously by such as the DTI, the Bank of England and various registrars of financial institutions and vests these, along with wide-ranging powers, in the FSA.

The FSMA spells out four statutory objectives for the FSA:

- Market confidence – maintaining confidence in the financial system.
- Public awareness – promoting awareness of the benefits and risks associated with different kinds of investment.
- Protection of consumers – securing the appropriate degree of protection having regard to differing risks and expertise involved.
- Reduction of financial crime.

While the details and specifics are comparatively new, the intentions are not. In fact, attempts to legislate against crooks and charlatans can be traced back to the 17th century. In 1697 Parliament passed an 'Act to restrain the ill practices of brokers and stock jobbers'.

If you're familiar with legislative and regulatory history, you'll know that it was not until the 'Big Bang' of 1986 that some of those practices were finally swept away, which just goes to show that investor protection in the broadest sense is a complex matter – it takes a long while and several attempts to get the desired result (in the UK at least).

Origins and focus of legislation

The aim of early UK legislation was, first, to outlaw and then to restrict the practices of stock-jobbing and broking. Subsequently, when it became apparent that much of the anguish and agony experienced by investors during the great depression of the 1920s and 1930s was due to fraudulent ramping of share prices and pressurised selling practices, the focus shifted to dealing with fraudsters.

Prevention of fraud

Two Acts with the same name – the Prevention of Fraud (Investments) Act – were passed in the mid-20th century, one in 1939 the second in 1958. However brave the intentions, the effect of these Acts in regularising the various business activities comprising the investment industry was minimal, partly because of a lack of precise definitions of terms and partly because of the skill and ingenuity of the industry (and the fraudsters) in coming up with new instruments and techniques that the law had not anticipated.

After a number of scams and scandals in the 1970s and 1980s, an examination of industry practices, particularly those of the LSE, and a growing recognition of the import of European directives, led to the 'Big Bang' of 1986. 'Single capacity' jobbers and brokers gave way to 'dual capacity' firms and commission scales came tumbling down. The Financial Services Act 1986 (*FSAct*), implemented in April 1988, paved the way for a fresh approach to UK legislation with its focus on creating 'authorised firms' and making it a criminal offence to carry out investment business without being authorised.

Together with the EU's first *UCITS Directive* of 1985, the 1986 FSAct shaped our present laws and regulations governing the conduct of investment business and operation of collective investment schemes. When the Labour Party came to power in 1997, previously expressed dissatisfaction with the self-regulatory system established under the FSAct, and its failure to prevent the pensions mis-selling and Robert Maxwell scandals and the collapse of Barings Bank, heralded a sea-change to a more centralised and comprehensive framework, with explicit emphasis on senior management's responsibility for a firm's behaviour and control.

The FSMA came into effect at midnight on 30 November 2001, a previously unspecified date known as 'N2'[2] and replaced, among other legislation, the Financial Services Act 1986, which had been operative from

---

[2] 'N1' was in June 2001, when responsibility for supervision of banks transferred from the Bank of England to the FSA.

'A-day', 29 April 1988. Other legislation affecting (separately) banks, building societies, life companies and friendly societies, which was also a feature of the middle and late 1980s, has been incorporated into the FSMA.

Other European directives to have a significant bearing on UK investment businesses are the *Investment Services Directive (ISD)*,[3] which aims to provide the 'single passport' for EU investment firms to trade freely across Member states, and the *Capital Adequacy Directive*, which complements the ISD by specifying common minimum levels of financial resources to be maintained by firms taking advantage of the single passport.

In December 2001, the UCITS directive was amended to broaden application of the cross-border marketing permissions of existing securities funds to other types of fund, such as money funds and funds of funds, and, more recently, to widen the investment powers of all UCITS funds.

Another significant directive applicable to UK funds is the *Distance Marketing Directive*, which restricts telephone sales and similar dealings with investors at a distance and requires the issue of detailed information to investors before transactions can be completed.

For all practical purposes the primary legislation is the FSMA, which, as has already been explained, defines

---

[3] Scheduled to be replaced by the Marketing of Financial Instruments Directive (*MiFID*) in April 2007.

'investments' and 'investment businesses'. Its scope is the UK and, therefore, transactions concluded outside the UK are not covered by its provisions. It also excludes investments in collectibles such as antiques, stamps and works of art, as well as money lending (except loans secured on land, which are covered) and certain other purely financial transactions, which still are governed by separate legislation. It does, however, cover 'deposit taking' and its definition of 'investments' includes contracts of insurance and participation in Lloyd's syndicates.

The FSMA also defines the regulatory structure for the UK, placing responsibility on the 'designated Secretary of State' (currently the Chancellor of the Exchequer) and making provision for the establishment of a 'designated agency' to be responsible for carrying the legislation into effect (currently the FSA). A number of other government departments and agencies are important elements in the overall regulatory framework, particularly HM Revenue & Customs and the National Criminal Intelligence Service (*NCIS*) but also the Office of Fair Trading and the Panel on Takeovers and Mergers.

Other legislation bearing on the conduct of all companies carrying out investment businesses includes the:

- *Criminal Justice Act*, which among other things legislates against insider dealing.
- *Proceeds of Crime Act*, which provides the primary anti-money laundering legislation.

- *Companies Acts*, which govern the general conduct of a company's affairs and that of its directors.
- *Data Protection Act*, which lays down principles, procedures and rules for the holding by businesses of data about individuals.

For Stock Exchange listed companies, the *listing regulations* (issued by the FSA) lay down requirements and procedures for companies and their directors in relation to transaction reporting, announcements, dealings by directors in the company's shares, financial information, price-sensitive information, etc.

Another important non-statutory body is the Takeover Panel, which scrutinises transactions involved in a change of ownership of companies whose shares are held by the general public. It demands high standards and expects companies to comply with its Code of Practice, the *City Code on Takeovers and Mergers*, or the 'Blue Book'.

In its work, the Panel and, in its application, the Code have implications for other bodies, notably the Competition Commission, the Office of Fair Trading (*OFT*) and the EU Commission. The OFT has a significant responsibility to ensure the rulebooks of regulators are not anti-competitive, but unhelpfully can only exercise its powers after such rules are published. Hence, there was consternation and delays over efforts to introduce disclosure rules for non-life products in 1996.

Other codes that have a bearing on how fund management companies carry out their business are:

- The FSA's *Code of Market Conduct,* which provides guidance on what is and what is not 'market abuse' – a new offence under the FSMA and aimed at market professionals but also broadly applicable. It explains that 'market abuse' is any behaviour based on information about an investment that is not generally available and which
  - would be regarded as relevant to a regular user of the market when deciding on the terms for a transaction in that investment;
  - would give a regular user a false or misleading impression of the supply of or demand for or the price of the investment;
  - would be judged by a regular user as behaviour that would distort the market and to be a failure to observe the standards of conduct expected of market users.
- *The Combined Code,* which lays down principles of good corporate governance. Issued by the Financial Reporting Council, the code is largely aimed at reducing the powers of single board members, in favour of collective responsibility that is subject to scrutiny by independent non-executive directors. Examples include requiring the posts of chairman and chief executive to be held by different persons and that committees of non-executive directors be responsible for such matters as remuneration and internal audit.

Returning to the FSA, its areas of responsibility are far-reaching, in line with its statutory objectives. The FSA has published its *Handbook of principles* and detailed rules, guidance and evidential provisions, which displaces the rulebooks of the former SROs and introduces a new risk assessment approach to supervision and authorisation. The FSA is responsible for direct enforcement of the FSMA, including policing the outer perimeter or boundaries of what is or is not investment business; direct regulation of firms that obtain permission to engage in a regulated activity and what the FSA itself describes as 'system management', which includes maintaining central registers of authorised businesses and 'approved persons', conducting fraud investigations, monitoring for consistency across its rulebook on connected topics, especially new developments such as promoting via the Internet; and exchanging information and concerns with other regulators, within the UK, across the EU – where the FSA is a prominent member of the Council of European Securities Regulators (CESR) – and globally.

Firms that conduct investment business only as an ancillary activity, such as firms of accountants or lawyers, may be authorised to do so by the relevant Designated Professional Body (DPB) – e.g., the Institute of Chartered Accountants, the Law Society. If the extent of financial services activity is material (usually taken to mean providing more than 50% of the firm's revenue) then authorisation must be sought from the FSA.

Organisations whose investment business is the running of a stock exchange or similar investment market are exempt from the FSMA's requirement that investment businesses must be authorised by the FSA, but instead have to acquire, from the FSA, status as a

Recognised Investment Exchange (*RIE*); firms transacting business on a foreign exchange are subject to different FSA rules when the exchange is designated as offering comparable facilities and protections with those in the UK – Designated Investment Exchange (*DIE*) – and those which are not. The former transactions are referred to as being 'on-exchange' and the latter as 'off-exchange'. Firms offering services as clearing houses must acquire status as a Recognised Clearing House (*RCH*).

Regulation in practice

Effective regulation requires a system of cradle-to-grave relationships between the FSA and regulated firms and a mechanism for the protection and/or compensation of investors.

The regulators' first task is to scrutinise applications for authorisation and to be satisfied that the applicant meets the 'Threshold Conditions' laid down in the FSMA and covering the location and legality of the business venture, its resources – financial, system and human – in terms of adequacy, competency, probity as appropriate, and, generally, whether the directors and key officials are fit and proper people to conduct investment business. In particular, the FSA will assess the likelihood of failure of the applicant firm and the impact of such failure on achievement of its statutory objectives. Each firm is notified of its 'risk rating' – A, B, C or D, with A being the highest and D the lowest.

A much closer regulatory relationship is promised to firms rated A than those rated D.

Once firms are authorised, they must comply with all applicable rules and laws, provide periodic information on their business activities, including financial information, maintain specified levels of financial resources, keep records as prescribed and ensure the continuing fitness and propriety of officers, competency of all personnel and adequacy of business systems and procedures. The FSA has specified a number of activities that comprise the management and control of a firm as 'controlled functions' and may be carried out only by 'approved persons' – i.e., approved by the FSA. Approved persons are subject to a code, similar principles to those specified for the conduct of the firm's business and to requirements of honesty, competence and financial soundness. A key obligation of all regulated firms is that of 'treating customers fairly'; another is to ensure that all staff are competent to carry out their assigned duties.

All firms are potentially subject to periodic inspection visits from the FSA, but under the risk-based approach to supervision, the firms most likely to experience regular visits will be those assessed as posing high risk to achievement of the FSA's objectives were they to fail – the category A firms. These are identified by an initial assessment followed by a confirmatory visit under the FSA's ARROW[4] project.

---

[4] **A**dvanced **R**isk **R**esponsive **O**perating Frame**W**ork project.

Firms subjected to inspection visits – when the FSA will send a team from its Supervision Department to examine the records of firms' activities, to test for compliance, to test for existence and adequacy of key procedures, records and documents and to interview key personnel – are required to deal openly and honestly with the regulator and to co-operate fully. A report is issued subsequently and if deficiencies are identified, these must be remedied in the fashion and within the time agreed.

If deficiencies are significant or if the firm fails to respond to findings in the desired fashion, the matter may be referred to the FSA's Enforcement Division for further investigation and para-legal examination, which can result in censures, warnings, fines or withdrawal of permission to carry out regulated activities or some combination of all of the above. There is always the possibility that such referral produces vindication for the member firm and no action by the FSA, but disciplinary procedures are typically invoked only when the regulators are sure of their grounds. The firm is usually liable for the FSA's costs as well as the penalties it imposes for confirmed transgressions.

In extreme cases the FSA may pursue action against individuals it judges responsible for an infringement or malfeasance, particularly those registered as approved persons and charged with the proper management and control of the firm. In these cases, the FSA can seek imposition by the courts of a jail sentence as well as its more familiar penalties of fines and withdrawal of approval.

For firms showing a consistently good record of compliance and whose failure would have minimal impact on achievement of the statutory objectives, the FSA applies a 'lighter touch', characterised by infrequent visits and more informed desk-based monitoring (versus its predecessors' checklist/tick the box approach). Such firms may not experience inspection visits at all or only if the FSA discerns industry-wide problems or seeks to gain a comprehensive appreciation of particular business 'themes'.

All regulated firms must consistently adopt high standards of documentation of and adherence to procedures that are robust, efficient and designed to deliver compliance. Further, the staff and officials, especially those who are individually registered as approved persons carrying out controlled functions with particular investor protection dimensions (salesmen, investment managers, directors and such), must be suitable for their post, adequately trained and, if necessary, supervised and demonstrate continuing competence, integrity and compliance. Firms must also have in place good systems of compliance monitoring and be able to demonstrate that such monitoring has routinely occurred and has been effective. Finally, firms must have policies and procedures that allow employees to disclose or expose malpractice or wilful non-compliance confidentially and without fear of recrimination – 'whistleblowing'. The FSA imposes these requirements through its statements of principles for businesses and for approved persons, and of the responsibilities of senior management for the firm's governance, systems and controls.

As far as the investor is concerned, in addition to the general protection afforded by all of the aforegoing, the regulations provide further specific protections or remedies in the event of dissatisfaction or worse.

There are rules covering:

- the occurrence and conduct of unsolicited calls by company representatives seeking to make a sale;
- the making and dealing with investors' complaints;
- the provision of cancellation rights or cooling-off periods;
- payment of compensation in the event of proven loss due to incompetence or fraud;
- the provision of key information to investors, initially to allow an informed decision, and periodically to allow a regular assessment;
- the advertising and promotion of investments, prescribing the permitted content and style of advertisements, which must be 'clear, fair and not misleading'.

Non-compliance with these rules by a regulated firm is a serious matter and complaints from investors can lead to regulatory action against the firm in the same fashion as those identified by the FSA or by the firm's own compliance function during its routine monitoring.

ESTABLISHING A FUND
Who wants one and why?

The caption is intended to provoke rational thinking about the motivation for a manager to establish a new fund. Much of what has been said before now points to the answers.

The manager must either perceive or be aware of sufficient investor interest in a fund designed for a particular purpose and/or with particular investment objectives. In economic terms, either the manager is 'demand led' or the investor is 'supply driven'.

Before embarking on the detailed and potentially costly project of establishing a fund, the manager will want to have a pretty good idea of investor response and may well conduct market research to this end, both with the investing public and with institutions and advisers.

This research or known demand will indicate whether the fund will appeal to the retail market – i.e., the general public – or to the wholesale market – i.e., institutional investors – and this will be significant in terms of marketing costs, investment approaches, and policies toward pricing and charges.

Other factors to be evaluated include:

- The duration of the fund – is it to be closed-ended and with a fixed future liquidation date or is it to be open-ended with no fixed duration?

- The primary investment objective – is it to produce capital growth or high levels of income?
- Taxation – what are the tax implications for the fund, the investors and the manager?

Options and approaches

We have already discussed the different types of fund and their principal features and advantages, and an early decision must be made about the most suitable type of fund for the venture under consideration. Other associated considerations will include availability of suitable trustees/custodians for the underlying investments and the facilities for dealing and settlement on the markets on which they are traded.

The manager must then decide the need for and form of overt marketing of the fund. It may be that little effort is required beyond informing interested investors and providing them with the relevant documentation. Many new funds designed to facilitate major underlying investment are pre-sold in this way. Conversely, retail funds tend to require extensive promotion both directly and through intermediaries, principally via presentations, mailshots and media advertisements.

The regulations governing the chosen type of fund must be understood fully, as must the regulatory process, to actually achieve establishment and authorisation to market the fund.

Then, as before, the specific tax requirements and positions of investors must be considered in detail and this may well cause a re-examination of earlier decisions or indicate whether the fund should be established in the UK or in an offshore location.

Whilst the tax treatment of a UK fund and of its UK resident investors may produce no compelling reason to avoid such treatment, an offshore regime may not tax income or gains locally and, by agreement with the UK authorities (who may offer reciprocal arrangements), the investor can defer tax on income or gains until remitted to the UK. These can be powerful incentives to establish offshore. If there is perceived to be substantial investor interest in or near the offshore location, then that would probably confirm the fund to be an offshore fund.

It used to be the case that the type of fund most favoured by investors (particularly non-UK investors) either as a result of its suitability or because of familiarity – i.e., the open-ended investment company – could not be established in the UK and so the decision about type could also determine location.

The UK became more attractive with the advent of OEICs and even more so since the amendments to the UCITS Directive, which the FSA has carried through into more liberal rules.

In theory, within the EU, managers operating UCITS should be able to freely market their funds across Member state borders, once obtaining a confirmation from the host state authority. The FSA has shown itself rather more willing to follow this particular feature of the Directive than some of its European counterparts and so a significant number of funds that had been located offshore by UK managers, for structural reasons, became the subject of application to the FSA for recognition and permission to sell into the UK.

Similarly, managers have routinely established funds (particularly, money funds) in the Channel Islands and other designated territories for tax reasons, and then obtained recognition from the FSA. UK resident investors can then enjoy the tax advantage of interest being retained in the fund and not distributed and thereby taxable in the UK – so-called 'roll-up funds'.

Use of the Internet for marketing to and dealing by investors makes physical location less of a consideration for managers, but raises obvious issues for regulation of firms and funds operating via the World Wide Web.

Documents and authorisations

Whilst jurisdictions will vary in their detailed require-ments, funds designed to be marketed to the public will require to be authorised for that purpose and the process follows a similar pattern in most countries.

Documents which establish the fund's constitution as a trust or a company – together with a prospectus or equivalent document describing the fund's purpose, objectives and policies, its charging structure and other operating arrangements – are submitted to the relevant authority together with a marketing plan, a fee and a formal request for authorisation.

The relevant authority in the UK is the FSA and its process for the authorisation of a unit trust or OEIC exemplifies the general requirements of most authorities. A prescribed form of application providing basic details – of the fund and of the manager/ACD, the trustee/depositary, the investment adviser (if applicable), the auditor and any other party to whom either the manager/ACD or the trustee/depositary will delegate functions – is submitted with a draft copy of the constitutional document (trust deed or instrument of incorporation), the scheme particulars or fund prospectus, a plan describing how and where units/ shares will be marketed, a solicitor's certificate confirming the constitutional document complies with FSA requirements and a cheque for £610 being the FSA's current fee for considering applications for authorisation of a fund established in the UK.

IMA has developed model documents for use by UK managers and the FSA is known to be favourably disposed towards applicant firms that adopt these documents with minimal change.

Launching the fund

'Launch' denotes the initial offer of units or shares in the fund to investors. Usually, this takes place at a fixed price for a fixed period, the length of which is typically limited by regulations and, in the UK, cannot exceed

21 days – i.e., 'days' not 'business days'. Promotion and marketing is at its most intensive during this period as the manager wants to achieve a critical mass of funds under management as quickly as possible, so that portfolio construction is facilitated and fund expenses are kept to a minimum per unit/share.

Depending on local regulations, market conditions or the success of the launch, the manager may invest the money subscribed during the launch period either on receipt or at the end of the period, and awaiting the end of the launch period is likely if the manager has set a minimum subscription level. Before launch, the manager will also want to ensure that all of the necessary administrative and management procedures and systems are in place, operational and able to handle the anticipated volumes. This will apply to both the fund and the management company itself.

Chapter

3

. . . .

PORTFOLIO MANAGEMENT

Strategies, styles, objectives and policies

Rather like economists, fund managers all have their own pet theories and, hence, their preferred style of portfolio management. Whilst there are plenty of wrong ways to go about managing other people's money, there is no single right way, and 'you do it your way and I'll do it mine' sums up the welcome reality that not everyone thinks or acts the same way. If they did, aside from there being no fun in the world, there would be no markets in investments!

What the professional fund manager has to do is strike an appropriate balance between risk and reward, as required by the investors or beneficiaries of the fund in his or her charge, and to operate within such constitutional, legal or regulatory constraints as may apply.

Whilst any categorisation is simplistic, it is the case that managers' basic styles can be described as either *top down* or *bottom up*. Another categorisation is between *active* and *passive* fund managers.

Top-down advocates start with economic analysis, to identify, first, prospering or soon-to-prosper national or regional economies; then, the industries or areas of business activity that will benefit from that prosperity; and, finally, the individual companies that will, in consequence, enjoy profitable growth.

Conversely, bottom-up advocates start by seeking out well-managed companies; then, they carry out detailed analyses of companies' performance and prospects as a basis for their investment decision.

The active or aggressive fund manager regularly makes changes to the fund's portfolio, in response to analysis of information, news and research, whether on individual companies or about national or international events or affairs.

Turnover of a fund's portfolio must be examined routinely to ensure the benefits of active management are not outweighed by dealing and administration costs nor cited simply to justify excessive activity, particularly if there are some ancillary fees or commissions being earned by connected parties. Regulators, including HM Revenue and Customs, have a keen eye for 'churning' or excessive dealing, which may not be in the investors' best interests and may prejudice tax concessions on the treatment of a fund's capital gains.

The passive manager, in contrast, makes changes only in response to some pre-established criterion, such as a change in the constituents of an index used as a benchmark for portfolio performance. A *tracker fund* is a perfect example of passive management and requires no particular investment skills – its portfolio mirrors the index constituents. Variations on passive/tracker themes abound and a common variant is a portfolio which invests in all constituents of an index but not in the same proportions as the index – this is known as *tilting* the portfolio towards the more favoured stocks.

Investing by way of a fund is meant to provide not just the benefit of pooling individual stakes, but also a reduction of risk by way of a diversified portfolio. Herein lies a dilemma for both investors and fund managers. Funds can be high risk, even though they have a diversified portfolio, because of concentration on or specialisation in an industry or country.

Regulatory requirements, if applicable, will limit the extent of holding in any one company and of any one company, but if the investment is a successful one, such limits will also restrict the fund from participating fully in that success – i.e., the upside is limited – unless all stocks in the portfolio perform equally well.

Meeting investors' requirements

Most people would like to 'get rich quick' and demand nothing more from their investments than high reward with low risk – i.e., loads of income, tremendous capital growth and no likelihood of loss! Which, of course, if not cloud nine, is certainly 'cloud cuckoo land!'

It should be recognised that people have different needs at different times, and that even the same person has a spread of needs that will change over time. However, a basic requirement for all investors is to convince themselves that they know:

(a) the relationship between their need for current income versus that for a future capital sum; and

(b) their appetite for risk in relation to their desire for reward – the twin emotions of fear and greed.

Adventurous attitudes may be tempered or inhibited by a concern for others or for the environment. People may choose their investments on ethical/ecological grounds as well as for financial reasons, and people investing with dependants or legatees in mind will likely take a cautious approach.

Taxation is an important consideration also, and the sophisticated investor will evaluate the post-tax returns from alternative forms of investment before making a decision, although investments justified purely on tax grounds run the risk of adverse changes in tax legislation.

Sensible expectations can have an investment response via a fund, and advisers need to understand their clients' requirements before recommending any one particular fund. Here, I am referring to publicly available retail funds. If the fund in question is a pension or life fund, investors' requirements are known or pre-determined and individual profiles taken into account by actuarial methods.

Risks to be managed

From the investors' viewpoint, there is always the risk of fraud and deception. Glib salesmen and ramped-up share prices are nothing new and investors must be sensible and alert to these risks. Examples regrettably abound –

from the South Sea Bubble to Barlow Clowes, Robert Maxwell, Nick Leeson and Peter Young, and from home income plans to personal pensions and split capital investment trusts. In only some, but far from all, of these cases were investors greedy or stupid.

Another risk for the investor is choosing an incompetent fund manager. Honesty alone is not enough and the best of reputations for integrity can be tarnished by accusations of incompetence. A third risk is of paying too much for the service or performance delivered. Value for money is the aim, not necessarily cheap, which may turn out to be dear in terms of the long-run performance.

The fund manager carries a responsibility to be as sensitive to the investors' perceptions of these risks as he is to the investment risks of his portfolio.

By definition, funds reduce risk by the simple fact of being a portfolio comprising a number of investments, spread or diversified across different asset classes and economic sectors. From the manager's viewpoint, his risks, assuming integrity and general competence, relate to the portfolio and his decisions to make changes. They include receiving poor-quality information – i.e., information that is not or cannot be verified as being accurate or reliable – and/or the judgmental risk of placing the wrong interpretation on the information (or not spotting the flaws).

Portfolio performance is always exposed to the risk of adverse economic news and events, and fund managers must, first, evaluate and, then, respond appropriately to news of changes to interest, tax and FX rates, as well as to news about or affecting individual companies, industries, sectors, countries or regions.

All managers run market risks, which is to say that the processes adopted by stock markets around the world vary from one to another and, therefore, create differing degrees of risk as regards liquidity, settlement, registration of ownership and custody of stock.

Even if all these risks are well controlled or managed, the fund manager still faces a major risk of mis-timing his investment decisions – timing is everything in investment. No one can consistently buy at the bottom and sell at the top, the aim being to avoid buying at the top and selling at the bottom!

Hedging

Fund managers avail themselves of various risk-management tools or techniques and one such is *hedging*. Most of us are familiar with the expression of 'hedging your bets'. Well, 'hedging' has much the same meaning in a fund management context.

Having decided on the optimum constituent stocks for his portfolio, the fund manager will, at various times, want to conserve, protect or lock in a profit, or trim, limit or insure against a loss. Hedging allows him to do each or all of these, as well as, in relation to stocks not yet purchased, to insure against a rise in stock prices.

The principal instruments utilised are *options*, which are rights, not obligations, to buy or to sell a fixed quantity of stock at a fixed price (the 'exercise' or 'strike' price) at some future date. Options are usually dated – i.e., they have a fixed life and, if not exercised, will expire. They may be in relation to a specific stock or to an index of stocks, when they are usually known as *futures*. They may also take the form of contracts which are themselves traded on a specialist market – e.g., Euronext.LIFFE – the London International Financial Futures & Options Exchange, now owned by the Euronext Consortium.

Options markets levy a fixed charge per contract, which, like payments for an insurance policy, is called a 'premium'. Futures markets also require buyers to put up a portion of the value of their contracts as part of the confirmation of trades procedure; this is known as a 'margin' and may be a one-off payment ('initial margin') or may require periodic adjustment depending on the changing value of the contract ('running margin'). Otherwise, settlement of trades is usually against delivery of stock or payment of consideration on pre-determined settlement or account days.

A fund manager wishing to protect his portfolio of UK stocks from a general fall in UK share prices could decide to purchase an index option giving him the right to sell to the market a quantity of contracts equivalent in amount to the value of the portfolio at the current level of a relevant index – say, the FTSE 100 index. If the market does fall, the value of his contracts will rise to compensate and he can sell the contracts to offset losses on the underlying portfolio. If the market rises or does not fall, the contracts will have no value and a small premium will have been paid for insurance against the uncertainty.

Similarly, a manager wishing to buy a particular stock in a rising market but without immediate funds could purchase an option to buy at current price levels. If the option is on the particular stock and its price rises, then the option is exercised directly; if the option is on the index, then the option is sold and the proceeds used to offset the rise in the stock price. If the price does not rise, the option contract is allowed to expire.

Index contracts are also used by managers to achieve a switch of investment exposure before changing the underlying holdings of a portfolio. This is termed *tactical asset allocation* and allows the manager to achieve a switch of economic exposure from, say, Japan to the USA by selling Nikkei–Dow index contracts equivalent in value to the Japanese portion of the fund, and buying S&P 500 index contracts in the same amount. This change in exposure is achieved without actually selling the Japanese stocks or buying the American stocks, trades which can be carried out over time, with associated unwinding of the options positions and without unduly alerting the market to the manager's policy, thereby avoiding the adverse effects of market price changes.

Another use of hedging (or *efficient portfolio management* as its broader use used to be described by the FSA with respect to the management of regulated collective investment schemes) is to provide an element of certainty, whereby profits can be 'locked in' and losses minimised on the actual holdings of stocks. Specialist futures and options funds are available and some are constructed with 90% in risk-free gilts or similar and 10% in index futures, thereby offering a measure of equity exposure but with near certain security of capital.

The FSA has adopted rules that impose different limits on the use of derivatives by regulated collective investment schemes according to whether the fund is or is not a UCITS fund or is or is not a retail fund. Although certain funds may devote their portfolios exclusively to derivative instruments, the rules for retail schemes such as unit trusts and OEICs essentially provide that derivative positions must be used for hedging rather than speculative purposes and that open positions must be *covered* by holdings of the relevant stock(s) or of cash. Other, non-retail and non-UCITS funds have greater freedom, provided the manager institutes a documented risk management process.

'Please don't ask for credit ...'

Gearing, borrowing and lending are related features of fund management that may or may not be available to the manager, or may be constrained by the fund's governing deed or equivalent, or by regulations.

'Gearing' is the term used to describe the extent to which a fund (or a company) has borrowed money to increase its investment portfolio, the rationale being that investment returns are greater than the interest cost of the debt over the period of the borrowing. The manager can thus squeeze more out of the fund by enlarging it.

The borrowing can be *structured*, as in the case of an investment trust which issues loan stock or a similar debt instrument, or simply short-term arrangements by way of a bank loan or overdraft granted in anticipation of future receipts. The amount of borrowing will be limited by the Financial Services Authority (*FSA*) if the fund is a unit trust or Open-Ended Investment Company (*OEIC*), by the articles of association if an investment trust and by equivalent regulations or constituting documents for other types of fund.

Other than lending by way of holding debt instruments – such as gilts or bonds – funds are not typically lenders in the manner of banks. Indeed, retail funds sold to the general public are not allowed to lend money. They are, however, permitted to lend stock, provided it is fully covered by collateral and an undertaking to re-instate the stock is given by the borrower.

'You can't do that!'

To obtain the continuing benefits available to funds, the manager must observe specific restraints on his freedom of management. Regulators don't want to stifle expertise or innovation, but they don't want managers running wild in their management of funds bought by the general public. Similarly, HM Revenue and Customs will root out abuse of the tax concessions granted to the various funds if its conditions are not met.

The first and most obvious constraint is that the fund must be invested in accordance with its objectives as stated in its constitutional documents. If the fund is set up and marketed as a Japanese Ethical Smaller Companies Fund, then the manager is not free to purchase shares in companies incorporated outside of Japan, no matter how good a thing they are.

Similarly, either the constitutional documents or regulations will prescribe the markets that are deemed 'eligible' for the fund's investments, and set down rules for both diversification and concentration of holdings.

The FSA's rules for retail unit trusts and OEICs – both UCITS and non-UCITS schemes – follow the Undertakings for Collective Investment in Transferable Securities (*UCITS*) Directive in requiring managers to pursue a policy of prudent spreading of risk; more detailed rules limit the amount of a fund that can be invested in the securities of any one company to 10% and those that exceed 5% cannot aggregate to more than 40% of the fund's Net Asset Value (*NAV*). To prevent concentration, the rules prohibit an authorised fund from holding more than 10% of the amount in issue of another company's capital of a particular class.

Investment trusts are limited by HM Revenue and Customs rules to 15% in any one other company.

Other trustees, including pension fund trustees, are governed by the Trustee Act 2000, which imposes a duty of care in making investments and keeping trust investments under review. In practice, institutional funds will rarely be troubled by the provisions of this Act, as their investment policies are both comprehensive and comprehensively set out in their deeds.

Asset allocation versus stock selection

I forget to whom I should attribute the admonition 'Give your decisions, never your reasons; your decisions may well be right, your reasons will invariably be wrong', but it seems appropriate enough for the art of fund management.

Asset allocation is really the process described earlier of a top-down approach to selecting investments, whereby a set of desired percentage holdings in various economies, sectors or industries are established at the outset and portfolio management consists of complying with those parameters or obtaining approval for deviation.

Stock selection is where the bottom-up approach starts and where any approach ends up.

Tactical asset allocation has a more precise meaning as discussed under *hedging*.

CHOOSING THE INVESTMENTS
'First, pick your markets'

Markets are a feature of everyday life and have been for centuries. Wherever there is a significant demand for food and other commodities there is likely to be a market. Some are general markets, catering for all requirements and tastes; others are specialised, dealing only in one commodity or in connected goods only. In London, familiar markets are at Petticoat Lane, Smithfields, New Covent Garden, Spitalfields and Borough High Street.

Markets have existed for some while also for metals and for stocks and shares. London examples again are the International Stock Exchange, the London Metal Exchange (*LME*) and Euronext.LIFFE, as already mentioned. Whilst the structure and modus operandi of these may not appear much like the food and general markets, the underlying principles and features closely compare. A distinction is that, whereas general markets tend to be open to the public as buyers, financial markets tend to be restricted to members, who will most likely operate in a dual capacity as both buyers and sellers.

All markets have certain generic features and individual markets will have more or less detailed operating practices, settlement procedures and regulations, depending on the type and value of the commodities being traded. Terminology to describe the participants may vary, but markets require buyers, sellers, brokers and market-makers.

It is the physical and operational features that tend to distinguish one market from another, 'physical' meaning its location, housing and size in terms of area occupied. There are essentially two distinct styles of operating in a market.

The traditional market operates an 'open-outcry' system, whereby traders shout out prices for their goods, in the hope of attracting responses from buyers, who accept or ignore the traders' quotes. This is somewhat akin to an auction, although contracts are made each time a price is accepted rather than when the bidding has reached its highest. Among UK financial markets, the LME is one of the few to cling to this method.

A quieter variant on this style is the familiar market where stallholders display their goods and prices, making occasional announcements of special prices or news. The old London Stock Exchange operated in this way when it was housed physically in the Stock Exchange Building and comprised jobbers and brokers as its members, each operating in a single capacity – jobbers as principal traders, brokers as agents for their investor clients.

Nowadays, financial markets tend to operate electronically with participants in their individual offices connected to each other via computer terminals linked to a central system, which displays price information, disseminates news and processes agreed trades. The London Stock Exchange operates in this way and, with the introduction of CREST, has moved significantly towards a totally electronic trading and settlement system environment.

As markets become increasingly computerised, so the period between trade date and settlement date shortens. A few years ago, practice in London was for settlement to occur 1 week after the end of 2- or 3-week account periods, which gave splendid opportunities to play the market with little money. Nowadays, settlement must be within 3 days of the trade date ($'T + 3'$). In the gilt market, same or next day settlement is the norm.

Markets tend to specialise in the different physical, financial and investment instruments – i.e., money, currencies/foreign exchange, commodities, metals (both precious and non-precious), securities and derivatives.

Portfolio weightings and profiles

Having settled on the markets, the fund manager then needs to decide the basic structure and appearance of the portfolio.

The manager adopting a top-down approach will probably develop an *asset allocation model*, wherein desired percentage exposures to countries, currencies and industries will be pre-set. From this the stock model will be derived, showing the desired holdings in individual securities. The bottom-up manager will not have an asset allocation model but may have a stock model or model portfolio.

Introducing some terminology and conditions, portfolios which deviate from or have a mismatch versus their models are said to be *overweight* in holdings or exposures where actual exceeds model in any respect, and *underweight* in opposite cases.

Portfolios that have no spare cash are said to be *fully invested* or to have *nil liquidity*. Whilst the preferred position of fund managers is to be fully invested, this can be a problem for the successful open-ended fund manager. As such funds attract more and more investment, so it becomes harder for the fund manager to increase holdings in chosen stocks, either at all, if there are insufficient shares in issue of chosen companies or without forcing up the price, or to find alternative stocks without raising the risk profile of the fund. Conversely, funds with large positions in stocks, particularly of smaller companies, find it difficult to switch holdings or realise their investment without depressing prices.

Income and growth

From the investor's angle, it is really a case of *you pay your money and take your choice*, but from the fund manager's angle, the relative emphasis to be placed on these typically non-complementary prime objectives will determine the composition of the fund's portfolio, subject to risk considerations. If the emphasis is on income generation, then the portfolio will tend to have a high proportion of its value in high-yielding shares and fixed interest stocks, whereas a growth-orientated portfolio will concentrate on equities in companies with good records of business growth and re-investment of earnings. It is possible to have, if not the best of both worlds, some of each, and 'balanced funds' aim to achieve a reasonable level of income and of capital growth.

Larger funds, particularly life and pension funds, would tend to sub-divide the total fund into sub-funds with different emphases or objectives – e.g., a portion of a pension fund could be managed as a sub-fund to produce the necessary income for pensions in payment and be invested in gilts or property, whilst another portion could be managed to provide maximum growth for its younger members and be invested in equity growth stocks.

Liquidity

I have already mentioned the manager's normal preference to be fully invested.

However, most funds will have a need for a degree of liquidity, if not in actual cash, then in near-cash or readily realisable assets, in order to pay the various charges and to provide for 'pay-outs', be they pensions, claims on a life fund due to death or maturing policies, or simply redemptions of shares or units in an open-ended retail fund.

Also, as discussed, it is sometimes a mistake to be fully invested and managers will from time to time decide that the time is not right to invest fresh money or that 'going liquid' is the best response to market conditions or news. This conscious decision by the manager can be referred to as *tactical liquidity*, and can be seen in evidence, for example, just prior to a major new issue of shares, when managers who wish to have a position in the company concerned will realise other holdings to release cash for the new investment. This may also occur when a manager wishes to take up the fund's entitlement under a rights issue.

For retail funds, managers are obliged to state their liquidity policy in their formation or marketing documents, so that investors may have advance knowledge of how the manager may respond to certain events and so change the invested/uninvested profile of the fund.

Evaluating alternatives

Whatever approach is adopted, eventually all fund managers reach the *make your mind up time*, when decisions have to be made about buying and selling the stocks of individual companies or other issuers. There is a variety of decision-support systems available and it is to be hoped that the mere toss of a coin is not much in use!

As in other walks of life and in respect to other types of purchase, how to make major decisions in investment is a mixture of intelligence, in terms both of information and common sense, analysis and having the courage of your convictions. Except for funds with the narrowest of investment policies, there is an enormous range of alternatives to choose from, and the first requirement is to be able to sort the wheat from the chaff, so to speak.

Is past performance a guide to the future? Clearly not in picking the winning lottery numbers! The regulators of retail funds think not, requiring advertising literature to carry warnings to the effect that past performance is not a guide to future performance and that the value of your investment and the income from it can go down as well as up. However, it must be argued that if a company has managed its business successfully for a number of years, it would be naive to disregard the possibility that it will continue to be successful. The same should be true of fund managers, although, of course, few investors know who is actually taking the decisions about the composition of a fund's portfolio.

When it comes to the history of share prices, a whole near-science has grown up about the shape of their graphs, and *chartists* are people who rely upon their interpretation of these graphs and their extrapolation into the future to guide their investment decisions. Many managers are self-professed chartists and one cannot dismiss this approach out of hand. What charts may offer is a guide to how markets react at key points or in response to major news or events. Since prices are the result of market activity, therein may lie the validity of the chartist approach. Certainly, entire businesses have grown up to service the chartists.

The natural protagonists of non-chartists are *quants* –

people who engage in detailed quantitative analysis of fundamental data about the companies and the markets and look for numeric absolutes and trends to support or suggest investment actions. With the power of modern computers and the general fascination with data, quants are much more in evidence today than heretofore.

Prominent among early quants was Jim Slater, whose method of using 'value filters' to identify companies with share prices at a discount to their proper value (as he saw it) used to be available on subscription to a hefty weekly publication – *Company REFS*. Slater's approach is more widely described as 'value investing' – seeking out companies whose market price is less than the 'right' price determined by fundamental analysis of the companies' prospects. Another quant approach is 'growth investing' where a purchase is made following analysis, regardless of the current market price.

Not all fund managers fall naturally into any of these 'camps'. One of my acquaintances dismissed them all in rather colourful language, claiming that all you had to do was watch the dealing screens to see what's happening to prices in the market and then *'Buy what's going down and sell what's going up, as long as you do neither to excess in case the market has got it right!'* I doubt whether such an approach would serve him well in all market conditions or with large institutions or discerning investors, but I cannot deny he was successful. Perhaps he just didn't want to share his more scientific methods!

It's worth mentioning at this juncture that the use of numbers and value analysis has led to a phenomenon known as the *programmed trade*, generated automatically by the manager's computer system (designed to filter and analyse all relevant data) when it detects that certain pre-set conditions prevail. The widespread use of such systems has been cited as the cause of major market movements, skewing the normal balancing effect of willing buyers and sellers towards one-way trading.

Another manner of trading based upon analysis is 'limit trading', when an order is placed to buy or sell but only if the price meets advised parameters. An example would be 'Buy ICI if the price falls to £x or less' or 'Sell ICI if the price reaches £y or better'. Such trade instructions would not be executed unless and until the price conditions were met.

Whichever style or technique the manager favours, the successful manager will be one who also applies qualitative judgments concerning a company's:

- management and its stated aims and policies;
- product strengths;
- customer base – size and loyalty;
- suppliers – number and dependencies;

all of which affect sustainability of its earnings and, hence, its share price.

Data, ratios and measurements

Quants will argue that *'It's all in the numbers'* and it would be foolish in the extreme to ignore key data about the companies whose shares are being considered for investment, about the markets on which those shares are traded and about the portfolio being managed.

Company data that provide indications of health or otherwise include:

- volumes of sales or turnover;
- gross margin or mark-up on sales;
- size/length of the order book;
- absolute and relative amount of costs and overheads;
- NAV and, particularly, the ratio of net current assets to liabilities, referred to as the 'current ratio' and the 'quick ratio' when stock is excluded;
- budgets for research and development and product development;
- Return On Capital Employed (*ROCE*).

Market data that may have a bearing on the investment decision include:

- capitalisation – i.e., the total value at current market prices of the company's shares in issue;
- the highs and lows of the share prices over selected periods;
- the ratio of share price to Earnings Per Share (*EPS*), known as the 'Price/Earnings ratio' or 'PE ratio'; may be expressed to be historic or prospective (*PPE*);

growth in the PE ratio features strongly in Jim Slater's approach (*PEG*);

- dividend yield, actual historic and current estimated;
- comparisons with equivalent data about companies in the same sector;
- volumes of shares traded from day to day – an indication of how readily the shares can be bought or sold at quoted prices and of likely dealing spreads between buying and selling prices;
- directors' dealings – reported information that is seen by some as an indication of faith or otherwise in the company by its management; seen by others to reflect a shift towards remunerating key executives with share options.

Portfolio data that must be factored into the decision-making process include:

- actual versus desired spread of investments – diversification;
- current weightings versus stock and asset allocation models;
- income yield – crucial for income funds but less important than total return for others.

At this point, I should perhaps mention both the perfect market theory and the Capital Asset Pricing Model (*CAPM*), as both have their supporters among fund managers.

The theory is that in a perfect or efficient market, all relevant information is known to all participants – buyers and sellers – at the same time, and, therefore, prices are always 'right', perfectly balancing supply with demand and without any opportunity for arbitrage, defined as the simultaneous buying and selling of the same asset on different markets to take advantage of pricing differentials. This essentially sums up the attitude of the 'growth investor'.

CAPM both builds on this and recognises that, in actuality, differences between a company's share price as determined by analysis and as determined by the market do arise. Further, CAPM concludes that each share has a 'Beta coefficient' that conveys the extent to which changes in its price correlate to movements in the market generally. Strong correlation produces a Beta of 1; prices that move more extensively than the market generally have a Beta greater than 1, and prices that move in a less pronounced manner than the market generally have a Beta less than 1.

CAPM's conclusion – the 'Security Market Line' (SML) – also predicts that once the conditions of a perfect market prevail then the price of all companies' shares will plot on the line. This provides a technique for the value investor to determine whether current market prices are likely to rise or fall and the Beta coefficient gives an idea of what's likely to happen to a particular price in relation to general market price movements.

The mathematics and formula associated with CAPM and Beta are set out in Chapter 7.

Dealing with events

'Nothing stays the same forever' and the fund manager cannot sit back and relax once he has achieved a well-structured portfolio. He must respond to news, events and market reactions, restructuring or rebalancing the portfolio in consequence. Only if the fund is designed to replicate or track an index is the task of changing the portfolio determined externally.

Open-ended funds pose an additional challenge, as the manager has to contend with inflows and outflows of money, sometimes at unpredictable times and in unpredictable amounts.

Fund liabilities are normally predictable, particularly those to fund holders, such as pension payments, income distributions, life policy maturities. Similarly, liabilities on investments such as calls on partly paid shares, are capable of ascertainment, as are liabilities for expenses and charges, such as the manager's fee, trustee's fee, tax bill and so on.

Contingencies are another matter altogether. Usually, they are associated directly with the portfolio, such as payment for rights issues if to be taken up, the uncalled amount on partly paid shares, the payment due on exercising conversion rights, but there are other instances not so directly related.

Deferred taxation is one such, denoting that a provision has been made but the amount is not payable until some future time or upon some future event. This usually relates to timing differences between actual receipts and payments and dates due, but can apply to the interest element of bonds traded cum-interest, or where interest value is included in the price.

Although considered remote, there remains the contingency of failed settlement of transactions, the failure of counterparties and the possibility of bad debts and fraud. Even where redress is available, the fund could be out of its stock or money for some time.

An unpleasant and unwelcome contingent liability for certain funds is that of the manager being fined by the regulators for some deficiency or misdemeanour. Although the regulated entity is the management company, not the fund, if the former is not incorporated, then all costs, including fines, are borne ultimately by the account or policy-holders.

News and announcements

Events external to the portfolio are primarily associated with or reported in company announcements or other general news items. In stock markets, it is highly questionable that *no news is good news* and it is more likely the case that no news is bad news for the condition of the company in question and, hence, your investment in it.

Markets thrive on information and prices move based upon interpretation of news and other information, whether good or bad. If information is sporadic, irregular or sketchy, then prices are likely to be more volatile and the spread between buying and selling prices will be wider.

General news items affect industries and economies and the same item of news may bode well or ill for individual companies – fund managers must be on the alert for opportunities for early purchases based on good news and for the warnings to sell signalled by bad news.

Think about, for example, what happens to markets generally and, then, to individual share prices of companies operating in different economic or industrial sectors following a major catastrophe, such as an earthquake or closure of a major airport that has suffered major structural damage. Initially, all share prices will be marked down by the market-makers but, gradually, as careful analysis identifies winners and losers, prices of some will recover and even advance. Emotional reactions to bad news have to be put aside and the successful fund manager is one who recognises and capitalises on an uninformed response by the market. There may well be winners among construction companies and losers among travel firms and insurers.

Company announcements are especially important to fund managers and their timing is regulated by the authorities running the market. This is to avoid a false market in the shares that could be caused when price-sensitive information is held by some participants only. In the UK and most other developed economies it is an offence to take advantage of information obtained on a privileged or insider basis and stock market authorities require companies to release information about results, dividends or other price-sensitive news promptly and to the market first. Market rules also ban dealings in the company's shares by insiders, particularly directors, for specified periods before and after major announcements.

New issues and underwriting

Like life itself, all securities began as a new issue, and new issues are special events in the life of a market and the management of a fund.

A company obtains a listing for its shares and makes a new issue for a variety of reasons, but mostly to raise new capital for the commencement or expansion of its business. When providing capital in this way, the market is described as the *primary market*. Trading in the company's shares, once the initial process of subscription and allotment has been completed, takes place in the *secondary market* or *after market*. Another term, used to describe pre-launch pricing by market-makers, is the *grey market*. If shares are to be issued to the public generally by open invitation to subscribe, the issue is said to be a *public offering*. If, alternatively, the issue is to be achieved by invitation only, typically to known institutional investors or large advisory firms for allocation to their clients, it is known as a *placing*.

The price of shares upon a new issue may be set in advance by the company, but may also be set *by tender*, which is to say that prospective investors are invited to state how many shares they would take up at a given price. When the application list is closed, the company reviews the tenders and settles upon a price at which the issue is fully taken up but which leaves some upward room for a healthy after-market. This price is known as the *strike price* and subsequent prices in secondary trading will be at a premium to (higher than) or a discount to (lower than) the strike price.

To avoid the costs and difficulties posed by a new issue not being fully subscribed by a public offering, most companies will take out insurance in the form of underwriting. Like the insurance market, underwriters of a new issue of shares will agree to take up an agreed portion of unallotted shares in exchange for an agreed payment, known as underwriting commission. If it is a large issue, then so-called lead underwriters who take on significant commitments may pass on some of their liability to sub-underwriters for a share of the commission. The risk to the underwriter is that the issue will fail to reach the stated amount and he will be 'stuck' with the unallocated shares, which in all likelihood will be worth less than the issue price.

Provided the regulations and the fund's investment policies permit, most funds will at some time or another underwrite a new issue, especially if it is by a company whose shares are desired for the portfolio. The principal constraint is that funds cannot enter into underwriting commitments if the potential holding would contravene either fund policy or regulatory limits on holdings. Provided those conditions are met, and the 'stick' can be avoided, commissions can be a useful form of supplementary income.

Rights, splits and scrip

These are special events, requiring special attention.

Unlike bonus issues, where a company issues new/ additional shares to existing holders by capitalising some of its reserves, a rights issue is a call by the company for further funds from its shareholders.

The conventional rights issue entails a provisional allotment letter, advising the shareholder that he has the right – but not the obligation – to subscribe for further shares based upon his existing holding – e.g., one new for every ten held. Payment terms will be specified and, usually, the price will be less than the prevailing market price to provide an incentive. The rights themselves, therefore, have an intrinsic value and prior to expiry will probably be traded on the market as a separate investment or entitlement.

Another form of right is the conversion right, which attaches most often to loan or debenture stock. Holders of convertible loan stock, for example, have the right to convert their holding into, say, ordinary shares at some future date or dates upon specified terms, which may or may not include provision for a further payment to the company. Similarly, warrants can be issued entitling the holder to subscribe to new shares by converting or exchanging a given number of warrants for ordinary shares according to a conversion formula, again upon prospectively favourable terms. Warrants are securities in their own right, but usually issued in conjunction with issue of another security – a bond or a share – 'with warrants attached'.

Sometimes a company adjudges that its shares are priced too highly in the market, and this is having an adverse effect on its ability to raise fresh capital on the primary market because the secondary market tends to become less active if prices go to too high a level. The response is to sub-divide the nominal value of the shares in issue (or split into smaller units) and issue extra shares to existing holders in the new denomination. Thus, a company whose 25p shares are trading at £5 each may decide upon a 5 for 1 split and re-organise its share capital into shares of 5p nominal. Existing holders will be notified that the number of shares now held is five times the previous holding and, other things being equal, the market price will fall to £1.

The corollary to this is when the company regards its share price as too low for it to be taken seriously – the so-called 'penny share'. If the price is seen as an impediment, then a consolidation of capital may take place, whereby, for example, ten old shares are replaced by one new one.

All shareholders have a right to income, assuming the company makes a profit and decides to distribute some or all of it. A method of retaining the distributable profit within the company whilst at the same time increasing the number of shares in issue is to make a *scrip issue*. *Scrip* is an alternative expression for *paper*, denoting that the company issues some documentary evidence of additional rights. In the case of a scrip dividend, holders are given the right to receive additional shares rather than cash.

Breaches of regulations

An unwelcome event in a fund manager's life is the discovery and punishment of a breach of the regulations which govern operation of his fund or of the management company that employs him. According to the regulators *'There's no such thing as an inadvertent breach'*; so few, if any, breaches can be explained away. Remember that fund management is a regulated activity and the fund itself may be subject to detailed product regulations, particularly as regards valuing, pricing, investment limits and marketing.

The FSA has set down unequivocal 'guidelines' for dealing with errors and breaches in the operation of retail funds. For example, errors in valuation and/or pricing of units in a unit trust which are equivalent to $\frac{1}{2}$% or more must be corrected by way of compensating the fund or unitholders as appropriate. The $\frac{1}{2}$% is a concession available to managers with essentially sound systems and procedures but which cannot be relied upon if there are repetitive errors or if the systems are inadequate.

Chapter

4

....

PORTFOLIO ADMINISTRATION

'Day by day in every way . . .'

Completion of this quotation from John Galsworthy's sequel to the Forsyte Saga runs '. . . we get better' or something like that. I suggest that 'administration' is the important day-by-day activity that must get better and, at best, be maintained at a high level of competence. Fund managers, or rather portfolio managers, could take a day off, even a week, and, although it would be unwise not to provide for cover, it would be most unlikely that a catastrophe would result. Not so with the administration department!

Buying and selling

The portfolio manager is in much the same position as any other investor, although he should be able to obtain finer rates of charge or commission on his trades, due to their comparatively large size. He will have to place his orders through a broker or direct with a market-maker and check whether his trade is being executed on a principal or agent basis. Trades through brokers are likely to be on an agency basis, with a commission charge; direct deals with market-makers will be on a principal basis.

The manager must ensure he is getting 'best execution' however the deal is placed – i.e., that the bid or offer price he obtains is the best available for the size and type of trade.

In addition to incurring commission charges on all agency trades, the fund will incur stamp duty on its purchases of UK shares. Stamp duty is the UK's oldest tax and is imposed in multiples of £5 for transaction values in successive bands of £1,000 up to £10,000 and, thereafter, at the rate of 0.5% or 50p per £100, rounded up to the next multiple of £5.

Delivery and settlement

Having bought or sold a security for the fund, the manager (as distinct from the portfolio manager, who could claim *It's not my job*) must arrange for the delivery of stock, if selling, or the payment of cash, if buying. The precise procedures will depend on the market on which the trade is executed, but, usually, the counterparties – i.e., the parties on each side of the transaction – are advised by the market authorities of their respective obligations and are expected to pay or deliver according to the rules of the market. If trading and settlement are electronic, then the whole process is achieved automatically.

For pension funds and unit trusts, the manager must advise the trustee of the fund to effect settlement, as it is the trustee who is the registered legal owner of the securities held by the fund. Similarly for an OEIC, the manager must advise the depositary or custodian.

Registration

Registration is a special area of administration and it is the entry on the register that provides evidence of legal title to the security in question.

I am referring here to the share or stock registers maintained by the issuing companies or their registrars, but the content and other requirements are identical to those applicable to registers of unit/share holders in a fund. The name that is entered on the register must be that of the legal owner of the security. In the case of most funds, this will be the trustee, depositary or custodian.

Registration details are usually provided at or soon after the time the trade is executed and automatically supplied to the company's registrar in the electronic environment or conveyed on a stock transfer form in the paper environment.

The date on which the relevant entry is made in the register is significant for the reason that it is on and from that date the fund becomes a 'holder of record' or 'registered holder' and entitled to the full rights attaching to the security, such as dividend or interest payments, or rights issues, or the right to attend and vote at meetings of holders.

If the trade occurs close to the date when the issuing company announces a dividend (its ex-dividend or xd date), then although the purchaser may buy cum-dividend, the register may not be updated in time and the seller receives the dividend due to the buyer. In these cases, provision is made for 'market claims' so that the buyer receives payment from the seller.

Custody

Registration and custody are closely related in that legal ownership of fund assets is usually carried out by an organisation that is independent from the manager who is operating the fund. When the registered holder is the trustee of the fund, it is almost invariably the case that he will also be the custodian – i.e., the person who is registered as the legal owner – and, unless the security is in dematerialized form, has physical possession of the documents of title held in safe custody for the beneficial owner. Also known as the *depositary* (as distinct from a *depository*, which is a warehouse or place of custody or storage), the custodian of non-UK securities may be the trustee or his overseas agent (if a bank, usually described as its correspondent).

Whatever the terms or practices, crucial to competent administration and control is regular reconciliation of records between the manager and the custodian, and periodic confirmations from the custodian that title to the stocks has been verified.

Use of nominees

A nominee is someone acting in place of another, and, in the context of investments, means the name on the register when it is not readily identifiable as the name of either the legal or beneficial owner. The reason for using nominees is largely administrative efficiency.

For example, if Barclays Bank is the trustee of the XYZ Growth Fund, the fund assets need to be registered as being in the legal ownership of Barclays Bank, but in a way which allows ready identification with the fund. One use of nominees is for Barclays to register any stocks held for the fund in a name such as 'Barclays Nominees Subaccount XYZGF'. If the fund holds foreign securities, Barclays may permit registration to be in the nominee name of its appointed agent, if local market practice means that this will facilitate future delivery.

Sometimes, particular forms of investment must be registered in a nominee name, the most common example being investments held via a Personal Equity Plan (PEP) or Individual Savings Account (ISA), which must be registered in the name of the plan manager, either solely or jointly with the plan holder.

In days gone by, nominees were frequently used to conceal the true ownership of securities from the issuing company, possibly for tax reasons or to conceal a holding being built up as a prelude to a takeover bid. Such concealment is restricted today by market rules and Companies Act legislation, which require notification of ownership of holdings exceeding 3% of the amount in issue.

As funds have grown in size and number, registration has become a major administrative responsibility, requiring significant investment in computer systems. The use of nominees today is as a convenient and cost-effective method of maintaining control, while facilitating delivery and settlement.

Stock exchange reporting

This is an aspect of administration more related to the listed company than to most funds, although if the fund is an investment trust then the FSA's listing rules will apply. As has been discussed, the fund manager must be aware of these rules and pay particular attention to instances of late reporting by companies or late announcements, which might presage bad news. The normal requirement to report trades to the stock exchange is fulfilled on behalf of the fund by the broker or marketmaker who effects the trades.

Records and regulations

The obligation of regulated firms to treat customers fairly includes being able to evidence:

- that allocation of any bulk trades between different funds has been fair (*whose?*);
- that the security and amount thereof are clearly identified (*what?*);
- that the trade has been executed promptly or in a timely fashion (*when?*);
- the reasons why the trade took place and why these explain 'suitability' (*why?*);
- that the price paid or obtained constituted 'best execution' (*what price?*).

These requirements are designed to provide an un-equivocal audit trail from thought to deed, and to demonstrate that the manager has carried out his business in an efficient and compliant fashion.

The records must be held for at least 3 years (longer if associated with money-laundering checks) and be open to inspection by regulators and, if applicable, trustees.

Portfolio accounting and controls

A fundamentally important aspect of fund administration is accurate and complete recording and accounting of transactions. These include unit/shareholder transactions, the investment transactions of the portfolio manager, and the associated income and expense transactions arising from holding the investments and managing the fund.

For the fund itself, the manager must maintain investment accounts which separate capital transactions from income transactions and can provide statements of gains and losses, both realised and unrealised, holdings and the movements in holdings and in cash coming into and leaving the fund, and current and comparative positions and valuations.

Various analyses and projections or forecasts are also called for, principally to allow tracking and adjustment of fund performance in relation to yield and income distribution targets.

There will also be an accounting requirement for the management company, in respect of its dealings in the units/shares of its funds (its 'box' profits and losses) and for its income from initial, exit and annual charges, net of discounts and commissions.

Controls over the fund's portfolio activity are required to demonstrate compliance with the fund's investment objectives and policies as set out in its deed or its equivalent constituting document and/or in its prospectus or similar document that describes the fund in detail to investors. In the absence of narrower restrictions in these documents, the limits contained in applicable regulations will prevail.

Typical limits will be concerned with the percentage of the fund's value that can be invested in securities of a single issuer and in unlisted securities, the percentage of the net assets of the issuer, liquidity levels, and the use of derivatives and other portfolio management techniques. There may also be regulations or restrictions governing the choice of markets that the fund invests in, and limiting the amount that can be invested in markets that are not deemed eligible.

Accounting controls will include regular reconciliations of records with bankers and trustees as regards the cash and stock positions of the fund's capital accounts, and of dividend and interest income on its income account. Confirmation should be obtained for all outstanding or unreconciled items or amounts and action to clear put into motion. Routine compliance monitoring will examine the effectiveness of these accounting functions, as will the annual audit. Only when all these procedures are in place can the firm claim that it demonstrably complies with:

- each fund's stated objective and investment policies;
- any regulatory or other restrictive limit on each fund's investments;
- best practice in operations and accounting.

Profits, income and taxation

Fund administration relating to the capital property of the fund requires the accurate and complete recording of portfolio transactions and positions for purposes of settlement, delivery, valuation, reporting, taxation and reconciliations with the custodian.

Portfolio transactions create realised gains or losses on the capital account. Revaluations of individual holdings produce unrealised gains or losses, and holdings of foreign securities and cash similarly produce gains or losses upon conversion into sterling, assuming that to be the currency of account.

Fund administration relating to income involves collecting the income on investments and interest on un-invested cash, together with any fees or commissions earned, and paying the expenses, charges and taxes. Detailed records of income must be kept to verify that all entitlements are received, only permitted expenses are paid, and net income for allocation to individual unit/shareholders can be determined with confidence, distributed accurately and reported on as required, including to HM Revenue and Customs of interest payments to non-residents, as required by the EU Savings Directive.

As regards taxation, practice varies according to the type of fund and according to the jurisdiction, but most jurisdictions treat the fund for tax purposes as a company whose ordinary business is holding investments, and only tax the income arising from that activity – i.e., dividends, interest, etc. – less expenses of management. There are variations, however, and the treatment of one type of fund should not be assumed to apply to other types or in other jurisdictions. For example a UK life fund will have a tax liability on capital gains, whereas a unit trust will not, provided the activity of portfolio management is not so active as to constitute trading in investments.

UK units trusts and Open-Ended Investment Companies (*OEICs*) are treated alike and pay corporation tax at the special rate currently of 20% on any surplus of un-franked income – i.e., any income other than dividends from UK companies – over management expenses. Against this liability may be set any foreign tax suffered on income arising from non-UK holdings. When it makes a distribution of income to holders, the fund makes payment to HM Revenue and Customs on account of corporation tax and the payment to the holder is accompanied by a tax credit of 10%.

If the fund has a significant portion of its income arising as interest, then it may treat its distribution to individual holders as an interest distribution. In this case, the tax accounted for by the fund is treated as a deduction of income tax and recipients of an interest distribution can offset or claim repayment of this amount. These comments apply to individuals; the position of corporate holders is different.

Other taxes that have a bearing on fund management are:

- stamp duty on the purchase of UK shares (and on the issue of new units or shares in the fund);
- stamp duty reserve tax on the purchase or issue of dematerialised securities;
- VAT on certain fees paid by the fund or the fund management company.

Taxation is a specialist topic and not a major component of this guide, but I hope I have covered the principles and some of the details.

Valuation and pricing

Whilst you may find it simply interesting to value your investment portfolio from time to time to see how much you have made or lost since last time, funds must prepare regular valuations as the necessary basis for determining the amount attributable to each participant and the price (or prices) to be paid to or by the manager when issuing units to incoming holders or redeeming units of outgoing holders.

Any such prices must be fair and reasonable and preserve equity amongst all participants remaining in the fund. This holds true regardless of the type of fund, but it is especially valid for open-ended collective investment schemes, which are continually issuing and redeeming units or shares in the fund.

The value of a fund largely depends on the value of its underlying securities and other assets, which, after deducting liabilities and expenses, is the fund's Net Asset Value (NAV). Regulations usually prescribe how and how often a manager must perform a valuation. The majority of funds are valued on a daily basis, but some managers prefer a weekly valuation, and some carry out more than one each day. The prospectus or scheme particulars of the fund will specify the valuation days and the time of day at which the valuation will be carried out, sometimes known as the 'valuation point'.

In most countries outside the UK, funds are valued on a single-pricing method and, although this basis is applied to UK OEICs, unless the Financial Services Authority (FSA) has a change of heart, it allows UK unit trusts to persist with a dual-pricing system, although the option to adopt single pricing is available under certain circumstances.

The steps in completing a fund valuation are as follows:

- multiply the number of shares held in each security by its market price(s);
- aggregate the value(s) of each investment thus obtained;

- add uninvested cash to give the portfolio or capital value;
- add income received/receivable;
- deduct expenses, charges and taxes, including provisions, to give NAV.

Buying and selling prices are then obtained by dividing NAV by the total number of shares or units in issue and, if applicable or permitted, adding or deducting the manager's charges.

Although shares or units generally are traded at a single price, regulations may require several prices to be calculated, each for a particular purpose. For example, the current UK unit trust dual-pricing model requires:

- *creation price* – the price based upon market-dealing offer prices of the underlying holdings and payable to the trustee for the creation of new units;
- *cancellation price* – the price based upon market-dealing bid prices of the underlying holdings and payable by the trustee on the cancellation of units;
- *buying price* – the price paid to the manager by incoming investors, usually the creation price plus the manager's initial charge;
- *selling price* – the price paid by the manager to outgoing investors, usually a fixed spread down from the buying price, but must not be less than the cancellation price minus the manager's exit charge, if applied.

The manager has considerable discretion as to where the actual buying and selling prices are set, provided the buying price is no more than creation plus the maximum rate of charge, and the selling price is no less than the cancellation price nor more than the creation price. This discretion will be removed if single pricing is adopted or imposed, although incoming or outgoing investors may suffer a dilution levy under certain circumstances to protect the interests of continuing holders.

There are also advocates of a 'swinging' or a 'semi-swinging' single price to ensure that continuing holders are not disadvantaged by large inflows or outflows that result in the fund suffering wide spreads on dealing in underlying securities – all highly contentious and the subject of vigorous debate.

Each price must be calculated to be accurate to at least four significant figures – which is not the same as four decimal places – and the most recently calculated buying and selling prices must be published each day in an appropriate manner, which usually is in at least one national newspaper but could be on the manager's web-site.

Controls and checks throughout this process are crucial. Apart from generating inequality among unitholders, errors in valuation or pricing must be examined and reported to the trustee and those greater than $\frac{1}{2}$% may require compensatory action.

Chapter

5

....

INVESTOR ADMINISTRATION

Agents, agreements and delegation

Regulations define a basic division of duties and responsibilities between the fund manager and the trustee or the depositary/custodian and prescribe that these parties must be independent of each other.

This is to provide basic investor protection by separating the prime functions of making investment decisions from the physical custody and registered, legal ownership of those investments.

Consequently, although the regulations recognise the commercial sense of either party delegating certain functions, they prohibit either party from delegating its prime responsibilities to the other. Thus, the trustee cannot appoint the manager its custodian and the manager cannot appoint the trustee its investment manager.

For a trust that assigns responsibility to the trustee for maintenance of the register of unitholders, the trustee can, however, delegate and appoint the manager the fund's registrar; similarly, managers frequently appoint third-party administration companies to carry out all tasks except investment management.

The need for specialist registration services can be illustrated by considering a fund with 100,000 unitholders, not an especially large register by today's standards. According to the statisticians, in an average week some 25 holders will die and some 200 will change their address, necessitating controlled changes to the fund's register. That's without considering the amendments resulting from the buying and selling of units.

This latter practice of delegating has become known as 'outsourcing', and as funds grow both in size and in numbers of investors, the demands for powerful computer systems are such that a discernible trend among new entrants to the market is to do little more than lend a brand name to the fund.

Overall responsibility cannot be delegated, of course, and even the most respected brand names must be able to satisfy the regulators of their understanding of investment business and their ability to select and monitor any third parties acting on their behalf. In practice, provided there is no abdication of responsibility, or delegation in such a manner as to give rise to a conflict of interest, a trustee/depositary and a manager/ Authorised Corporate Director (*ACD*) can organise matters in a way that is administratively most convenient, cost-effective and commercially sensible.

Outsourcing demands clear and comprehensive agreements, and preferably with explicit requirements for service levels. These latter are sometimes expressed in a separate Service Levels Agreement (*SLA*), operation of which is monitored for compliance as assiduously as the firm's own operations.

Investor transactions

The most significant transactions entered into by investors are the buying and selling of shares or units in the fund, sometimes referred to as *dealing*. Dealing in open-ended funds is usually carried out through the manager, who is normally acting as a principal in the transaction, buying or selling units on his own account and choosing whether to cancel or re-issue units redeemed. For unit trusts and Open-Ended Investment Companies (*OEICs*) the manager/ACD is not allowed to run a short position, but must create at the relevant time sufficient new units or shares to fulfil buying orders.

Procedure may require, at least for the first purchase, a written application form and may require payment in advance (mandatory if the fund is to be held in a PEP or ISA). Selling instructions are usually accepted over the telephone or by letter but will require submission of a form of renunciation of title to the shares/units being redeemed, which may be on the reverse of a certificate if issued or on a separate form.

Settlement is carried out by the manager once the required details and documentation are complete. Regulations set out requirements for unit trusts/OEICs as regards minimum times in which the manager/ACD must pay monies to the trustee/OEIC for new units/shares and to redeeming holders for units/shares being redeemed or repurchased by the manager, but timing of payments due to the manager/ACD from incoming investors is a matter for the manager's terms of business.

If the fund is closed-ended – an investment trust, for instance – its shares are usually listed and traded on a stock exchange and dealing and settlement are then carried out in the same way as for shares of other companies – i.e., through a stockbroker and in compliance with the Financial Services Authority (*FSA*)'s Conduct of Business and/or Listing Rules.

Relevant to dealing and settlement are the Client Money Rules, whereby monies received from investors that are not to be applied to the purchase of units/shares within 24 hours must be held in a separately designated client money account by the manager until the purchase is made and settlement is due.

Other points are:

- 'consideration' is the amount due on the purchase of an investment, and 'net consideration' means the amount including any charges and after any commissions or discounts;
- 'proceeds' is the amount due on the sale of an investment, and 'net proceeds' means the amount after deduction of any charges;
- contracts or contract notes are normally issued for lump sum investments, confirming all relevant details of the investment; investments made by regular contribution are usually confirmed by periodic statements;
- certificates or similar documents providing *prima facie* evidence of title to units/shares may be issued but, increasingly, funds are becoming 'dematerialised' or 'uncertificated', except for bearer shares/ units.

Registration

True generally except for bearer shares and true especially for uncertificated funds, the register of holders is the only legal proof of title to the shares/ units – a register is a formal record of the legal ownership of the shares/units issued by the fund.

The registration function is usually performed by the manager or an appointed registrar or transfer agent. In the case of a trust, responsibility is agreed between the trustee and the manager but, for a company, it may be performed by the company itself or delegated, either to the manager/ACD or to a specialist third party.

Details recorded should include:

- the name and address of the holder;
- the number and type of shares/units held;
- the date on which the holding was registered.

Transactions and action by the registrar are principally the adding and deleting of holders and the amendment of holdings, as a result of issues, redemptions and transfers between holders. Additionally, the registrar must update the register for conversions from one type of unit/share to another, switches between funds or sub-funds, splits or sub-divisions of high-value units, and, of course, changes in the personal details of holders.

These latter data are the subject of the *Data Protection Act* in the UK and no more data than is necessary for the purpose should be contained on the register. Similarly, changes to or enquiries about data held must be subject to disciplined procedures to ensure no unauthorised access or amendments to data.

Dates are important because entitlement to reports, income and other rights is granted only to 'holders of record' at a given date, usually an accounting date. The registrar normally updates the register and makes the holder a holder of record only on information received from the manager, and the manager is unlikely to confirm details until he has been paid for units/shares issued or received all necessary registration details.

It is normally the responsibility of the registrar to organise the preparation of income payments and tax vouchers and their despatch to holders, together with the manager's reports.

Communicating with investors

Throughout the time an investor is registered as a holder in a fund, there will a be number of situations requiring the manager to communicate with the fund's registered holders. Most are driven by laws and regulations, which apply both routinely but also to situations arising because the manager wants to change a material aspect of the fund's purpose or operation, and may require a meeting of holders.

Reports

Reports covering the fund's performance over the period since the last report are the most routine communication and are sent out within a short time after the associated accounting date. The contents comprise an investment commentary, formal accounts and notes to the accounts, together with other useful or relevant information to enable the holder to understand how the fund has been operated, the results of the manager's efforts and to base a decision on whether to maintain or increase the investment.

Managers may opt to provide short reports and/or short-form accounts, provided they make full versions available on request.

Distributions

Distributions of income call for specific communications, which comprise a cheque or warrant (or an advice if mandated to a bank) and a tax voucher.

The income of a fund constituted as a trust must be wholly applied for the benefit of the holders and must, therefore, be distributed or re-invested (net of expenses) by the end of each annual accounting period. The taxation aspects have been discussed earlier.

Changes

Changes made or proposed by the manager should always be advised to holders and certain changes may require their approval. Typical subjects of change are the investment objectives or policy, the name of the fund, and the amount or treatment of charges. Fortunately for investors, the regulators regard changes to objectives, policies or charges not contemplated by the original or current fund documents as fundamental changes to be implemented only with the approval of holders in a meeting called for that purpose and the prior approval of the regulators and, if applicable, the trustee. Other changes may be 'significant' and can only be implemented with prior notice being given to holders or in accordance with previously disclosed notification procedures.

Charges

Charges are a special case. A manager is usually able to increase the current level of charges up to the maximum level stated in the fund documents, subject to giving appropriate notice to holders and revising the current fund prospectus or equivalent. Proposed increases beyond the maxima stipulated in the fund documents are normally required to be presented to a meeting of holders for approval, but newer funds may be able to increase charges paid by the fund via the giving of notice of at least 60 days.

Fund mergers

Fund mergers also call for meetings of holders, usually only of the discontinuing fund. The manager must set out the reasons for the proposals in a formal document accompanying a notice of meeting and provide holders with details of the continuing fund, sufficient to enable an informed decision to be made by a reasonable person. Disclosure rules have application here also.

Conversions

Conversions of unit trusts into OEICs or into sub-funds of an umbrella OEIC are subject to a special procedure, but, nonetheless, require notification to trust investors and approval.

Meetings

Meetings of holders called for any of these purposes are conducted according to normal laws of meetings, but may also be subject to provisions of regulations applicable to the type of fund: 14 days notice is usual and quorum requirements vary according to whether the fund is constituted as a trust or a company and, if a trust, whether it is subject to the FSA's latest rules. A trust operating under the 'old' rules requires 10% of holders of record, at a given date and eligible, to attend and vote. This excludes the manager and his associates, unless they are the registered holder on behalf of another (such as a PEP, ISA or savings plan holding) and the beneficial holder has provided voting instructions. A trust operating under the new rules requires the representation of just two unitholders, in line with the quorum requirement for meetings of OEIC shareholders.

Resolutions for any fundamental change are presented as extraordinary resolutions, which means that a specified majority of votes must be cast in favour of the resolution before it is deemed to be passed, usually 75% of the votes actually cast. Voting can be in person or by proxy and can be by show of hands or, more usually, on a poll, whereby holders vote in proportion to the value of their holding.

FSA rules provide that an investor has no obligation to attend or vote at meetings, nor to vote all of his holding or to vote his holding all in the same way. These are necessary rules to cater for nominee holders who have to obtain voting instructions from the beneficial holders, who may not all give instructions, or, if they do, some may be to vote 'for' a proposed resolution and some 'against'.

If the fund is constituted as a company, it may be that applicable regulations or the constituting documents call for Annual General Meetings (*AGMs*) at which, like any other company, the annual accounts and other matters are presented for holders to adopt. AGMs are not required for unit trusts, and, therefore, the meetings described above are usually referred to as Extraordinary General Meetings (*EGMs*).

Trusts and OEICs may, nonetheless, call general meetings if the manager/ACD finds it useful or desirable. The normal meetings procedure applies.

Chapter

6

PERFORMANCE
MEASUREMENT

This chapter and the final chapter deal with assessing the absolute and relative performance of a fund, and, hence, of a fund manager. This chapter presents the theories and simple expressions; the next covers the more complex mathematics.

Sector comparisons – 'my fund is better than your fund'

One common measure of a fund's performance is to compare it with other funds competing for investment. There's no shortage of financial publications and data providers to feed the appetites of those who enjoy league tables. Although data on private or wholly institutional funds are unlikely to be exposed to public gaze, the absolute and relative performance of retail funds over various time periods can be found in any number of newspapers and journals, occasionally with entire supplements given over to, for example, an analysis of life company funds supporting endowment assurance policies, or investment trusts, or personal pension funds, or unit trusts.

Rarely are comparisons made between different product types, although unit trusts and investment trusts often come in for comparative scrutiny from time to time. It is a reasonable presumption that, if the decision to opt for a particular type of investment vehicle was valid when made, it remains valid and, therefore, the pitfall of comparing apples with oranges should be avoided.

The purpose of sector comparisons is to provide some assistance to the investor seeking to compare like with like. In other words, pension funds with other pension funds, life funds with life funds and so on. Within these broad classifications, sub-divisions can be made. The managed fund versus the self-select, the 10-year endowment policy versus the 25-year policy. Still finer divisions can be made based upon investment objectives and policies.

It should be noted in passing that the FSA's rules for funds established prior to 2002 specified nine categories of collective investment scheme for purposes of distinguishing types of retail funds according to investment policy – i.e., the type of underlying investments the fund is to hold. These categories provide for a mixture of very broad funds (i.e., securities funds) to very narrow funds (i.e., property funds), so cannot generally be used for comparisons of performance.

Classifications by industry is familiar from a review of share prices, as published in most newspapers. This is typically more useful than an alphabetical presentation or listing in order of price or market capitalisation. Presenting by sectors such as banks, media, engineering allows investors to compare the share price performance of one company with that of other companies engaged in much the same business. This classification not only permits like comparisons, it also provides a simple information tool to assist stock selection, reducing the likelihood of inadvertently being overweight in or overexposed to any single sector.

The trade bodies for retail funds – IMA for unit trusts and OEICs, AITC for investment trusts – have each defined performance categories into which their members' respective funds are classified. These classifications are based upon investment objectives – e.g., growth, income, balanced – but they also distinguish funds according to geographic emphasis – e.g., European, North American, emerging markets – or other criteria – e.g., smaller companies, fixed interest, funds of funds, property. The Investment Management Association (*IMA*) has some 30 such categories covering nearly 2,000 funds and sub-funds.

Statistical analysis of each fund's performance over various time periods is itself a business, or at least a part of related businesses. For example, Standard & Poor's Micropal and Hindsight provide most publishers and, indeed, fund managers, with data for performance comparisons. Mostly, the presentations are from an investor's viewpoint – i.e., the total return over a selected period if the investment were realised at the end of the period and any income arising during the period had been reinvested. The usual description is 'offer to bid, income reinvested'. Investors and potential investors should exercise care when considering these statistics. Published data may not be representative of personal experience or actions because the data assume lump sum investment at specified prior points in time, and not additions or regular contributions.

Similar services to investors or fund-holders are provided in other fields. The actuaries Towers Perrin produce a periodic review of pension funds, and the trade journal *Money Marketing* runs annual surveys of the performance of life company products.

Yields and returns

The same English words often have different meanings, according to where they are spoken. In my experience, it is also the case that *yield* means different things to different people.

The basic definition is reasonably consistent – i.e., a measure of the amount of income arising from the investment, expressed as an annualised percentage of the cost of the investment:

$$\frac{\text{Income for year}}{\text{Investment cost}} \times 100\%$$

This is commonly referred to as the income yield. The difficulties arise when the definition of the numerator is varied. If we wish to know the *historic distribution yield*, then the amount would be the total income received over the immediate past 12 months. However, we might be more interested to know the likely yield for the current calendar year (*current yield*) or the likely future yield for the next 12 months (*forecast* or *prospective yield*).

Each of these is a valid measure and the investor or prospective investor must choose the measure suited to his or her purpose. Similarly, a fund manager needs to look at dividend yields on the shares held in the fund's portfolio in each of these ways when evaluating alternatives.

Another variant on yield is the *portfolio yield*. This is sometimes called the 'portfolio's internal rate of return', and it represents the expected future annual income to be generated by the portfolio, expressed as a percentage of the current Net Asset Value (*NAV*) of the fund on a buying basis, thus:

$$\frac{\text{Future annual income of current portfolio}}{\text{Cost of buying portfolio}} \times 100\%$$

All of the above tends to relate to equity-based funds or funds without a preponderance of fixed dated stocks – i.e., securities that have a specified remaining life or duration to maturity, when the holders will be repaid on a specified basis. For such stocks and for funds holding such stocks, a relevant measure is the yield to maturity, or the redemption yield – i.e., the total return over the period held, expressed as an annualised percentage of the cost. The precise formula is rather complex but an approximation is given by the following:

Redemption yield or Yield to maturity =

$$= \sqrt[n]{\frac{\text{Interest income for the period} + \text{Maturity proceeds}}{\text{Initial cost/Current value of investment}}}$$

$$-1 \times 100\%$$

where n = the number of years to maturity.

Example

£1,000 nominal of a bond with a coupon rate of 10% maturing in 8 years' time produces £100 per annum interest or a total of £800 over its remaining life. If the purchase cost was £1,500 the running yield is:

$$\frac{100}{1,500} \times 100\% = 6.7\%$$

The yield to redemption approximates to:

$$\sqrt[8]{\frac{800 + 1,000}{1,500}} - 1 \times 100\% = \sqrt[8]{1.2} - 1 \times 100\%$$

$$= 2.3\%$$

The redemption yield introduces the notion of total return – i.e., the aggregate of income received plus capital growth over a stated period expressed as a percentage of investment cost or value at the beginning of the period. For investors building up a pot of capital rather than in need of significant income from their investment, total return is a far better measure of performance, both absolutely and for purposes of comparison with alternatives:

$$\text{Total return} = \frac{\text{Capital growth} + \text{Income for period}}{\text{Cost/Value at beginning of period}}$$

$$\times 100\%$$

A final variant is *index yield* which refers to the income return on a portfolio of the stocks constituting the selected index, most commonly the FT-SE 100 or the

FT-A All Share. This yield, calculated as an average of the dividend yields on the index shares, is a useful comparator for the yield of individual companies and also provides one component of a statistic known as the *yield gap*, and referring to the difference between that yield and the interest yield on a representative Government stock – traditionally $2\frac{1}{2}$% Consolidated Stock (*Consols*). In times of high inflation, the latter tends to exceed the former and is said to be negative or produce a reverse yield gap.

The terminology was based on the notion that investors expected the yield on more secure investments to be lower than on equities and, therefore, expected the gap to be positive. A negative yield gap was thought of as an anomaly, or a temporary phenomenon, and a signal to switch between equities and bonds. It is debatable how useful an indicator this is today, as more and more people regard equities as their preferred investment, even when dividend yields have fallen.

As has been shown, the components of a yield calculation will vary according to who is doing the measuring and for what purpose. On one aspect, however, most calculations are consistent – the answers are usually expressed as *gross* yields – i.e., before taking into account the investor's tax position. This is achieved either by using pre-tax amounts in the calculation itself or by engrossing the initial answer at the relevant rate of tax.

The first budget of the UK Labour Government elected in 1997 ordained changes to the tax position of certain funds, restricting their ability to recover tax credits on UK dividend income. This has severe implications for pension funds, both as funds and as investors, and for Personal Equity Plan (*PEP*) and Individual Savings Account (*ISA*) investors. Another consequence has been to cause a further 'spin' on yield calculations, since the gross yield will no longer be available to pension funds.

Time- and money-weighted returns

The commentary thus far has presented methods for measuring performance which take no account of the effect of money coming into or going out of a fund, yet for all but the most fixed, closed-ended fund, that is the reality. Neither have we discussed how to annualise a return for periods of less than a year.

The expression for calculating total return has been given above. Say, for example, the answer for a period of 1 month is 5%. To annualise this return, we assume that each month will return 5% and that we, therefore, need to employ a compounding method, since each month will start with an amount that is 5% larger than the previous month.

The method is to raise 5% to the power of 12, the convention being:

$$(1.05^{12} - 1) \times 100\%$$

which equals:

$$(1.7959 - 1) \times 100\% = 79.59\%$$

Realistically, an annual return approaching 80% is

rare indeed and an extrapolation that produces this result must be treated cautiously. Even so, this way of measuring total return is unsatisfactory if money has been added to or taken from the fund during the period. Such movements will have a positive or negative effect on the return calculated as above, as they will in and of themselves cause the fund to grow or shrink as a quite separate matter from investment performance. Consider the following funds:

	Fund A	Fund B	Fund C
Value to start	£1,000	£2,000	£3,000
Value at end	£2,000	£4,000	£6,000

On the face of it, each fund has returned 100% and, therefore, all three have performed equally well. But what if Fund B and Fund C had experienced an inflow of £1,000?

It would be tempting to say that Fund B turned £2,000 into £3,000 for an adjusted return of 50% and Fund C turned £3,000 into £5,000 for an adjusted return of 66%, but this would be true only if the inflow to both funds had occurred at the very end of the period. If the inflows had occurred right at the start, Fund B's adjusted return would be 33% and Fund C's 50% – i.e., Fund B turned £3,000 into £4,000 and Fund C turned £4,000 into £6,000. If the inflows occurred at any other, or at different, times or there had been several inflows and outflows, the calculations and, hence, the comparisons would be quite tricky.

Fortunately, mathematicians have provided a formula for dealing with this. It produces the 'money-weighted return' and requires the calculation and addition of returns for each 'mini-period' within the total period during which money flowed neither in nor out. The formula uses the Greek letter sigma (Σ) to denote this summing of returns and is quite complex, involving trial and error to solve. It is beyond the scope of this guide to do more than present the formula and suggest use of a scientific calculator or a spreadsheet! Using the following notation:

$$MV = \text{Market value of the fund}$$
$$\text{Cash}_T = \text{Cash introduced/withdrawn at time } T$$
$$T = \text{Proportion of period elapsed at time } T$$
$$\text{(e.g., 6 months is expressed as 0.5 of a year)}$$
$$R = \text{Internal or money-weighted return}$$

The formula is:

$$MV_{end} = MV_{start}(1 + R) + \sum \text{Cash}_T(1 + R)^{(1-T)}$$

Example

A fund worth £100m at the beginning of the year has an injection of £10m on 30 June and is valued at £125m at 31 December:

$$\text{Total return} = \frac{125 - 100}{100} \times 100\% = 25\%$$

The money-weighted return, R, is found from the expression:

$$125 = 100(1 + R) + 10(1 + R)^{(1-0.5)}$$

Substituting values for R, trial and error produces a money-weighted return of slightly less than 15%.

The drawback of the money-weighted return is that it only provides a valid measure of comparative perform-ance between funds that experience inflows and out-flows at much the same times. The timing and size of flows have a significant bearing on the money-weighted return.

The time-weighted return is designed to smooth out the distorting effect of cash flows by placing equal weight on the total returns for any single part of a period. This is achieved by calculating the return at each point when cash comes in or goes out for the period since the last movement and multiplying these returns together. Using the Greek letter pi (Π) to denote the product of a series of individual returns, the mathematical notation is:

$$R = \left(\Pi \frac{MV_{new}}{MV_{previous} \pm Cash} - 1 \right) \times 100\%$$

If, in the previous example, the value of the fund immediately prior to the introduction of the £10m was unchanged at £100m, the return for that first half of the year was 0.

The return for the second half was:

$$R = \frac{125 - 110}{100} \times 100\% = 13.64\%$$

The time-weighted return for the year is also 13.64%, calculated as under:

$$R = \{(1 + 0) \times (1 + 0.1364)\} - 1 \times 100\% = 13.64\%$$

This is a rather simplistic example, but it illustrates the point that time-weighted returns tend to be lower than money-weighted returns, which give an inflated measure of performance by not discounting the timing of cash inflows. The converse is also true, which is why time-weighted returns are preferred as performance measures. Also, they can be used to compare different funds with different experiences of cash movements.

Indices and benchmarking

So, with new-found mathematical expertise, we can demonstrate that our favourite fund manager is *absolutely fabulous*. The question remains, however, is he *relatively awful*?

Relative to what? Well, relative to similar funds obviously, but such comparisons are part only of the evaluation, which should include assessment against expectations or some quite independent measure. One such is a relevant index, such as the FT-SE 100. Constructing an index is covered in the final chapter.

For the moment, it is sufficient to examine what an index is and how it can be used.

An index measures changes over time. It does this by calculating the aggregate of the values of its individual constituents at a start or base date and expressing the result as a base number, usually 100 or 1,000. The aggregate values at a subsequent date are then expressed relative to the base date, as a multiple (or fraction) of the base number, thus providing a clear indication of the general level of prices or values of the constituents and whether this is rising or falling.

Consequently, an index can assist fund managers with the timing of investment decisions, by observed trends of prices as measured by the index and in the measuring of an individual fund's performance relative to the index. Clearly, the chosen index must offer a fair comparison – the constituents of the fund need to be similar to those of the index, or the index needs to be the fund's benchmark or target.

Indices can also provide a mechanism for constructing a benchmark portfolio according to selected asset allocations. For example, if the trustees of a pension fund of £100m stipulated at the beginning of the year a geographic asset allocation of UK 50%, USA 30% and Japan 20%, a benchmark return can be calculated using the movements over the year of the relevant indices – e.g., the FT-SE 100, S&P 500 and Nikkei–Dow. Let us say that the FT-SE had risen 20%, the S&P 25% and the Nikkei had fallen by 15% and there were no cash movements in the year and that the manager's total return has been calculated at 25%. Hence, the benchmark portfolio has grown from £100m to £114.5m and, therefore, returned 14.5%, calculated thus:

$$\{(100 \times 0.5) \times 1.2\} + \{(100 \times 0.3) \times 1.25\}$$
$$+\{(100 \times 0.2) \times 0.85\} = £114.5m$$

So, on the simple basis of total return, the manager has done better than the benchmark set by reference to selected indices in proportions which mirror the stipulated geographic allocation of the portfolio, and the trustees may be very pleased. However, before they can decide how good the fund manager really is, they ought to find out whether his outperformance is due to his skills at stock selection or to his deviating from the stipulated asset allocation percentages. If he has not deviated, then the outperformance can be said to be entirely due to superior stock selection.

Suppose that halfway through the year an extra £10m came in and the manager put it all into the US market instead of spreading it in the stipulated percentages.

A simple way of attributing the outperformance between the two possibilities is to construct a second benchmark, which mirrors the manager's decision to change the percentages from 50, 30, 20 to 46, 36 and 18 at the halfway point.

Without going through the calculations, if the value at year-end of this second benchmark is £118m, then, of the total outperformance, £3.5m (118 − 114.5) can be said to be due to asset allocation and the balance, £5.5m, attributable to stock selection.

This also answers the question of whether the manager's style was active or passive, since to have achieved such a superior return over the index benchmarks, he cannot have been passive! How active he has been cannot readily be judged from the example data; he may simply have selected index stocks but in a different proportion than the index – i.e., his tilting was in the right direction.

What the trustees finally want to know is how much risk the manager ran to achieve this performance, meaning did he take excessive risk – i.e., excessive to pre-established guidelines?

This requires us to examine risk and volatility a little more scientifically than heretofore.

Volatility and risk adjustments

Funds are exposed to risk because of uncertainty – about the cash flows that will arise from the investments made and about the market values of those investments at any particular time.

Although the assets depicted in Figure 6.1 start and finish the period at the same points, they display different volatility patterns.

Risk in this context means the likelihood of a share price being volatile, whether relative to the market

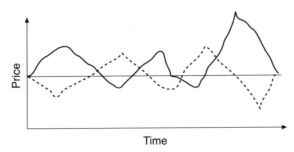

Figure 6.1 Volatility of prices over time.

generally, or within its own price range, and the frequency and extent of price movements over time.

There are principally two types of risk. One is the risk inherent in the entire market in which the fund is invested, termed *systematic risk*; the other is the risk that attaches to specific assets in which the fund is invested, known as *idiosyncratic* or *unsystematic risk*. Total risk is the sum of systematic and unsystematic risk, or, in American English, systemic and unsystemic.

The most common measure of total risk is the *ex post* standard deviation – i.e., how far the individual returns (or share prices or index values) deviate from their average value. Standard deviation measures the dispersion of individual values around the average of all values and, thus, is a measure of volatility.

A high standard deviation indicates large swings about the average and, therefore, a high level of uncertainty and, hence, high risk. Since the standard deviation of index returns can be calculated by taking a series of readings at, say, monthly intervals during the course of a year, this can be compared with the standard deviation of portfolio returns taken for the same intervals.

A comparison will reveal whether the portfolio is more or less risky than the index. This method can be extended to the benchmark portfolios constructed from different indices and provides a measure of the comparative risk profile adopted by the manager.

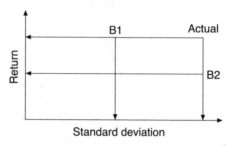

Figure 6.2 Comparison of the standard deviation of actual and benchmark returns.

In Figure 6.2, if B1 represents the profile of the benchmark portfolio, then, although the manager has achieved the same return for the selected period, the higher standard deviation means this is more volatile – i.e., less certain to be constantly achieved than is desired, and therefore achieved with higher risk that, for different periods, the return will be higher or lower than the range specified by the benchmark.

If B2 represents the benchmark, he has achieved a higher return for the same risk, which is most satisfactory, but, clearly, the star manager is the one who beats his benchmark by achieving a higher return and a lower standard deviation!!

More sophisticated measures are in use and these are discussed in the final chapter.

Chapter

7

. . . .

INVESTMENT
MATHEMATICS

In this final chapter, some of the techniques and measures presented earlier will be examined in greater detail and some new ones will be introduced. However, this is not a mathematical treatise! This chapter aims to describe and demonstrate some mathematically based approaches, to whet your appetite for analysis of funds closer to home.

The arithmetic of indices

We have already covered the general nature and use of indices and introduced the necessary terminology of base dates and price relatives. At times during the life of an index, it becomes necessary or desirable to *re-base* it, possibly because the start date is so long ago that the present levels are too high to provide meaningful comparisons. Re-basing requires selection of a new start date and a fresh calculation by reference to a selected base number at that date.

The three most common ways of constructing an index are arithmetic, geometric and weighted arithmetic. Remember that an index measures or reflects average price changes over time. The differences between these three types of index lies in the way they treat or ignore the size or volatility of individual constituents.

Simple arithmetic index

This is constructed as:

$$\frac{\text{Sum of prices at the current date}}{\text{Sum of prices at the base date}} \times \text{Base number}$$

or, in more mathematical terms:

$$\text{Index}_{cd} = \text{Base number} \times \frac{\sum \text{Prices}_{cd}}{\sum \text{Prices}_{bd}}$$

If the simple aggregate of prices of each share contained in the index at 1 January is £1,234 and at 31 December the aggregate is £1,345, we can choose 1 January as our base date, select 1,000 as our base number and express the 31 December index to be:

$$\frac{1{,}345}{1{,}234} \times 1{,}000 = 1{,}090$$

Examples of simple arithmetic indices are the *Dow Jones Industrial Index* and the *Nikkei Stock Average*.

Geometric index

This is constructed by multiplying together the current price divided by the base date price of each constituent share, taking the nth root of the answer (where $n = $ number of shares in the index) and multiplying the base number by this root.

The mathematical expression is:

$$\sqrt[n]{\prod \left(\frac{\text{Price}_{cd}}{\text{Price}_{bd}} \right)} \times \text{Base number}$$

Geometric indices are less sensitive to price changes of a single constituent share, but suffer from the flaw that if one share becomes valueless, the index becomes zero. Generally, they underestimate the performance of constituents and are not recommended for performance measurement. An example is the *FT Ordinary Index* of 30 industrial shares.

Using base number 1,000 and the following data:

Share	Price at base date	Current price	Ratio
A	36	39	1.08
B	127	158	1.24
C	95	90	0.95
D	260	300	1.15
Totals	**518**	**587**	**1.47**

the arithmetic index calculations produce an index at the current date of:

$$\frac{587}{518} \times 1{,}000 = 1{,}133.2$$

The geometric index calculation is:

$$\sqrt[4]{1.47} \times 1{,}000 = 1{,}101$$

Weighted arithmetic index

This is calculated like the arithmetic index, but uses the market capitalisation of constituent shares instead of share prices. Consequently, it places extra weight on those constituents that are larger companies. It is to be preferred over a simple arithmetic index, both as a guide to market behaviour and as a performance benchmark, because it removes the misleading consequence that a change in the price of a small company's share has an equal effect on the simple index as the same change in the price of a large company's share.

Examples are the FT-A All Share, the FT-SE 100, the S&P 500, each of which is an example of a Laspeyre Index – i.e., an index which ignores any capital changes and retains the base date weightings. An index which is re-based for capital changes – i.e., to current weights at the time of the change – is a Paasche Index. Each index is named after its creator.

Indices provide useful benchmarks for actual or absolute returns, but what about volatility?

Standard deviation

To remind you, standard deviation is a measure of dispersion of values around their own average and can be applied to returns, prices, ages and almost anything else that is meaningful to measure! The steps in calculating the standard deviation of a given set of data are:

1. Determine the arithmetic average, or mean.
2. Determine the individual differences from the mean (ignoring plus or minus).
3. Square each of the differences.
4. Sum the squares.
5. Divide the sum by the number of constituents (*less 1 if the set is not complete – i.e., it is a sample*).
6. Take the square root to return to the required unit.

Because the calculation is usually backward-looking when applied to investment situations, it is known as the *ex post* standard deviation and measures risk in terms of the volatility attaching to the item being measured. Large swings around the average for any single item whose values are measured at successive time intervals will produce a high standard deviation and indicate high volatility and, hence, risk. It is a fact that a minimum of two-thirds of values will fall within ±1 SD and 95% within ±2 SDs. 99% of values will fall within ±3 SDs, and this is usually depicted by a bell curve, so-called because of its shape (Figure 7.1). The vertical axis is more properly called the 'probability density function'.

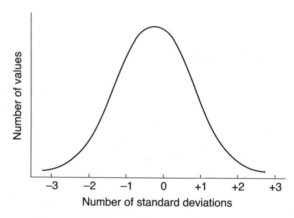

Figure 7.1   Distribution of variances.

A more sophisticated risk-adjusted rate of return is given by the Sharpe measure, which compares the portfolio returns measured at successive intervals with the returns from a selected risk-free asset for the same intervals. The latter is subtracted from the former and the answer divided by the standard deviation of the portfolio returns. The higher the resulting figure, the better, because either the fund is performing better than the risk-free asset or the standard deviation is low, indicating low volatility, or, possibly both. For example:

	Fund A	Fund B
Return	10%	10%
Standard deviation	3%	4%
Interest rate on gilt	4%	4%
Sharpe measure	$(10-4)/3 = 2$	$(10-4)/4 = 1.5$

In this simplified example, Fund A has the higher Sharpe measure and, therefore, is to be preferred over Fund B.

Capital Asset Pricing Model

The Capital Asset Pricing Model (*CAPM*) combines much of what has been discussed to this point, but uses a refined approach to risk assessment, in an effort to predict the behaviour of portfolios under given conditions at particular times and to assist in fund or stock selection to maximise returns.

It was developed by academics out of the so-called *Modern Portfolio Theory*, which emerged *circa* 1960. Although much-maligned in the UK, it remains very popular in the USA, largely because of the simplicity of its predictions. Detractors claim that this simplicity has been achieved at the expense of a realistic view of the actual workings of markets.

Assumptions and conclusions

The assumptions of CAPM are what cause the sceptics most difficulty. They are that:

- The market is perfectly competitive.
- There are no tax considerations.
- There are no dealing costs.
- All investors agree on:
  - the investment period;
  - the return expectations (ER);
  - the standard deviation of all assets.
- Investors can all borrow/lend at the same risk-free rate (R_f).

The conclusion is given the title *The Security Market Line (SML)* and introduces a measure known as the *CAPM Beta Coefficient*, which can be developed for a portfolio and also for individual shares as a measure of the systematic component of risk.

The expression for the SML is:

$$ER_{portfolio} = R_f + \beta(ER_{market} - R_f)$$

This last bracketed expression is the Market Risk Premium (MRP) – i.e., the difference between the expected return on the market and the return from a risk-free asset. The difference between the expected return on the portfolio and the risk-free return is termed the Portfolio Risk Premium (PRP).

Re-arranging the terms of this expression, we find that:

$$\beta = \frac{PRP}{MRP}$$

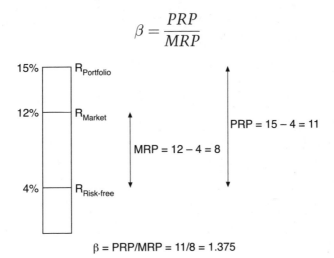

$\beta = PRP/MRP = 11/8 = 1.375$

Figure 7.2   Market and portfolio risk premiums.

and to illustrate (Figure 7.2):

$$\beta = \frac{PRP}{MRP} = \frac{11}{8} = 1.375$$

The Beta coefficient is calculated as the covariance of the return on the portfolio and the return on the market, divided by the variance of the return on the market. *Co-variance* is a mathematical term for the extent to which two variables move in sympathy. *Variance* is the square of the standard deviation. Calculations are beyond our scope!

If the portfolio returns move in an identical fashion to those of the market, the co-variance will produce a Beta of 1. A Beta greater than 1 denotes an asset that is more risky than the market as a whole, and a Beta less than 1 denotes an asset that is less risky – i.e., the return (or the share price) varies more or less proportionately to the return on the market (or the market index of prices).

Creating portfolios using CAPM

Portfolio Betas are calculated as the market value weighted average of the Betas of the individual stocks comprising the portfolio. The CAPM, or more precisely the CAPM Beta coefficients, can be used to create portfolios to suit specific risk profiles. For example, trustees of a pension fund with members nearing retirement would want a portfolio with a low Beta, whereas a younger, more adventurous investor could specify a high Beta.

A further example might be that of an ethical investor deciding on the percentages he should hold of two particular shares with Betas, respectively, of 1.5 and 0.6 in order to give a combined Beta of 1. To calculate the answer requires facility with simultaneous equations:

Let $x\%$ be invested in Share A and $y\%$ in Share B:

$$x + y = 100\%$$

and the desired result is for:

$$1.5x + 0.6y = 100\%$$

Multiplying the first equation by 1.5 and subtracting the second equation we establish that $0.9y = 50$ and, therefore, $y = 55.6$ and $x = 44.4$. Rounding gives the split required of 56% in Share A and 44% in Share B.

Another application of the CAPM is in stock selection, using its prediction that over time or all other things being equal, all assets or portfolios should plot on the SML (Figure 7.3).

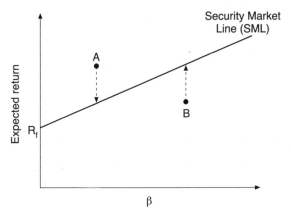

Figure 7.3 CAPM predictions

The asset's position on the chart is a function of both its return and its Beta. Given that return is calculated as known or expected earnings divided by current price, CAPM predictions mean that A's price must rise for its return to plot on the line, whereas B's price must fall so that its return is increased to plot on the line.

Treynor and Jensen measures

These are two further measures of risk-adjusted returns, which utilise CAPM Betas and, unlike the Sharpe measure, assume that unsystematic risk in a portfolio is eliminated by the large number or spread of holdings. This diversification permits the premise that only systematic risk remains – i.e., the general risk of the market (Figure 7.4).

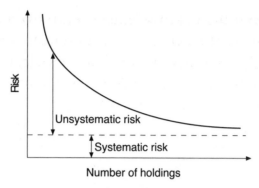

Figure 7.4   Effect of spread on risk.

The Treynor measure is that of the portfolio's excess return over its Beta and can be expressed as:

$$\frac{(R_{portfolio} - R_f)}{\beta_{portfolio}}$$

Using the earlier data of Fund A and Fund B, if their respective Betas were 1.5 and 0.9, their Treynor measures would be calculated as follows:

Fund A	**Fund B**
$(10 - 4)/1.5$	$(10 - 4)/0.9$
$= 4.00$	$= 6.67$

According to Treynor, Fund B now gives the better value, as its risk-adjusted rate of return is higher than Fund A's.

Whether Sharpe or Treynor provides the better measure is a matter of taste – Sharpe ignores market performance and selects according to the volatility of the asset's or portfolio's own risk premium – i.e., *PRP/SD*, whereas Treynor selects according to the relationship of the *PRP* to the *MRP*. Both can be shown to be the gradient of a line from the risk-free rate of return to the point of intersection of the actual portfolio return and its risk, measured by Sharpe in standard deviations and by Treynor as Beta. The steeper the gradient the better. This is illustrated with Fund A in Figure 7.5.

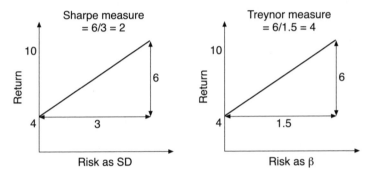

Figure 7.5 Sharpe and Treynor measures.

The Jensen measure utilises a benchmark portfolio with an identical Beta to the fund's portfolio. The difference in returns of the two portfolios is then taken to be the measure of the manager's skills (or otherwise) as an investor.

Sometimes known as the 'Jensen Alpha' the generalised expression is simply $R_{portfolio} - R_{benchmark}$. The higher the answer, the greater is the manager's skill. A straightforward example of its application is a calculation of the tracking error of an index fund, but 'alpha' is a measure widely favoured by fund managers to show how well they have beaten their benchmark.

GLOSSARY

. . . .

The following is not comprehensive; terms may or may not feature in the main text.

Accumulation units (UK) Units where net income is automatically re-invested.

Active management An investment management approach that seeks to outperform the market through the application of informed, independent judgment. The opposite of 'passive management'.

Advisor (US) The individual or organisation employed by a mutual fund to direct the investment and management of the fund's assets.

AITC Association of Investment Trust Companies, the trade association for investment trusts.

Alpha A measure of a manager's outperformance versus his benchmark.

Alternative Investment Market (AIM) (UK) The 'junior' market allowing companies to obtain a listing for their shares and trading via nominated brokers without the complete rigours of a full listing on the main market. Replaced the USM.

Annual charge A charge levied for the management of the fund.

Annual report A yearly statement of the financial progress and status of a fund.

Asked price (US) Price based on the Net Asset Value (*NAV*) plus sales charge, paid when purchasing shares (*see also* **Offer price**).

Asset allocation The mix of securities and other assets in which the fund's capital is invested.

Authorised unit trust (UK) A unit trust scheme authorised by the Financial Services Authority (*FSA*).

Automatic re-investment The use of income or realised capital gains for the purchase of additional shares or units of a fund.

Bear Someone who thinks a price will fall.

Bear market One where prices are influenced by sellers.

Beta A measure of the correlation of movement between the price of an individual asset and market prices.

Bid basis Fund prices are based on bid prices.

Bid/Offer spread The difference between the bid and offer prices.

Bid price The price paid under dual-pricing to holders redeeming their holdings.

Big Bang (UK) The change in the rules of the UK Stock Exchange which occurred on 27 October 1986.

Blue chip Shares in companies which are highly regarded, usually large and well established.

Bond A marketable debt instrument issued by a company or government.

Bond fund A fund that holds a portfolio that consists primarily of bonds.

Book or box Stock of shares or units held by managers acting as principals.

Bull Someone who thinks a price will rise.

Bull market One where prices are influenced by buyers.

Cancellation price (UK) The lowest price under dual-pricing at which managers may repurchase units, based on the bid prices of underlying investments.

Cancellation rights In certain circumstances an investor has the right to cancel a purchase of shares or units.

CAPM Capital Asset Pricing Model – used to assist stock selection; formula introduces Beta coefficient.

Capital gains distribution Payments to fund holders of their proportionate interests in realised gains from the sales of securities in the fund's underlying portfolio.

Capital Gains Tax (CGT) Tax payable on gains arising from the sale of securities.

Cash equivalent Short-term bonds, notes and repurchase agreements, usually government backed.

CESR Council of European Securities Regulators.

Closed-ended investment An investment company issuing a limited number of companies' shares.

Collateral Security pledged as guarantee of repayment.

Commission A fee paid by the manager to a third party such as an agent or IFA for introducing business.

Contract note Document sent to the investor when a purchase or sale is made, with details of the transaction.

Conversion factor (UK) The factor linking accumulation and income units.

Conversion of units (UK) Changing an investment from accumulation to income units, or vice versa.

CREST Electronic settlement system that provides registration and payment details for UK trades.

Cum distribution Includes the income distribution. The buyer is entitled to the next distribution.

Custodian A bank or trust company which takes custody of fund assets and securities for safekeeping.

Debenture Bond of company acknowledging debt and providing for payment of interest at fixed intervals.

Dematerialisation The process of ceasing to issue certificates to investors.

Derivatives Securities or contracts whose values are linked to, or derived from, other securities.

Distributions Payments of investment income or realised capital gains to fund share- or unitholders.

Diversification Spreading investments and risk among a number of securities and across different asset classes and sectors.

DTI (UK) Department of Trade and Industry.

Dual-pricing A system of calculating different prices for buying and selling units in a fund using market offer and market bid prices for the underlying securities.

Earnings The profit available for equity holders.

Eligible market A securities market in which a fund can invest.

Equity shares Shares in a company that are entitled to the balance of profits and assets after all prior charges.

Equities fund A fund that invests primarily in equity shares.

Ex-distribution (XD) or **ex-dividend (xd)** Excludes the income distribution or dividend. The seller is entitled to the next distribution or dividend.

Ex-distribution price (XD price) or **ex-dividend price (xd price)** A price that entitles the seller to the next income distribution or dividend, but precludes the buyer.

Exempt funds Funds for tax-exempt bodies.

Exit charge Charge levied on redemption of shares or units.

Feeder fund (UK) A relevant pension scheme dedicated to a single collective investment scheme.

Fiduciary Individual given the legal power to participate in the management of assets for the benefit of others.

Financial Ombudsman Service (UK) Deals with complaints against regulated firms.

Forward pricing (UK) Investors deal at the unit prices determined at the next valuation point.

Franked income (UK) Dividends received from companies out of their net profits after UK corporation tax has been paid.

Fund of funds (UK) A unit trust which may only invest in other unit trusts.

Futures and Options Fund (FOF) A fund that invests in approved and other derivatives (where most or all the transactions are fully covered by cash, securities or other derivatives).

Geared Futures and Options Fund (GFOF) A fund that invests in approved and other options derivatives (where most or all the investment is limited by the amount of property available).

Hedging The process of protecting a fund's assets from the effects of exposure to currency fluctuations or other investment risks.

Historic pricing (UK) Investors deal at the unit prices determined at the most recent valuation point.

ICVC (UK) Investment Company with Variable Capital – the regulator's preferred name for an OEIC.

IFA Independent Financial Adviser.

IMA (UK) Investment Management Association. The trade association for the unit trust industry in the UK.

IMRO (UK) Investment Management Regulatory Organisation Limited. An SRO under the FSAct 1986.

Incentive compensation A fee paid to the investment adviser determined by fund performance in relation to specified market indices.

Income fund A fund whose objective is to provide income on a regular basis.

Income units (UK)   Units where income is paid to unitholders.

Index fund   A fund that comprises or models the securities that make up the index being followed.

Individual Savings Account (ISA) (UK)   A method of holding investments without suffering tax on gains or on income.

Initial charge   Charge levied on investors when units in a unit trust are purchased (*see also* **Front-end charge**).

Initial offer price (UK)   The price at which units in a new fund are available to the public during the period of offer.

Initial yield   An estimated figure which indicates how much income a new fund might expect to receive in the first year.

Instrument of incorporation   The legal document that evidences the formation of an OEIC.

Interim accounting period   The period during which income earned by a fund is accumulated before payment to holders.

International fund   A fund that invests in securities traded in several different overseas markets.

Investment trust   A public limited company whose business is to hold and manage a portfolio of investments.

Key features   A document required by regulations governing disclosure of information to investors.

Liquidity   Part of the fund's portfolio held in cash.

Load (US)   A sales charge included in the purchase price.

Manager's box   *See* **Book or box**.

Market capitalisation   Total value of a company's issued securities at current market prices.

Management fee   The amount paid to fund managers for their services.

Money market fund   A fund which invests in deposits and other money-market instruments.

Mutual fund (US)   An open-ended investment company or trust which combines the contributions of many investors with similar objectives.

NASD (US)   National Association of Securities Dealers.

NASDAQ (US)   National Association of Securities Dealers Automated Quotations: a system that gathers, stores and displays quotations of trading prices.

Net assets   The total assets of a fund less current liabilities.

Net Asset Value   The value of the underlying shares held based on quoted (NAV) mid-market prices and other assets, less liabilities, divided by the number of shares in issue.

No-load fund (US)   A mutual fund with no front-end sales charge.

Nominal value   The face value of a share.

Nominee   A legal entity that holds shares on behalf of another entity.

Non-certificated   Shares or units for which no certificate is issued.

OEIC   Open-Ended Investment Company.

Offer basis   Fund prices are based on offer prices.

Offer price   The price paid by investors when buying shares or units under dual-pricing.

Off-the-page advertisements   Advertisements which appear in the press and contain an application form.

Open-Ended Investment Company (OEIC) (UK) Corporate form of collective investment scheme which issues shares at a single price based on NAV.

Par value   *See* **Nominal value**.

Personal Equity Plan (PEP) (UK)   An investment plan which is free of tax on any income or capital gain.

Periodic charge   *See* **Annual charge**.

Portfolio   The securities owned by a fund.

Pound cost averaging   For regular savings the average price per share or unit paid by the holder can be lower than the average price for the period in which savings are made.

Preliminary charge   *See* **Initial charge**.

Product particulars   Factual information about the investment.

Prospectus   The official publication which describes the objectives, policies, services, management, restrictions and charges (etc.) of a fund which takes the form of a company.

Purchase price   *See* **Offer price**.

Redemption price   *See* **Bid price**.

Registrar   The company which maintains the register of holders.

Regular income plan   Uses several funds to provide monthly or quarterly income.

Renunciation form   The formal transfer to the managers of shares or units being redeemed.

Rights issue   An issue of new shares to existing shareholders in fixed proportion to their holdings.

Sales charge (US) A front-end charge included in the purchase price of a mutual fund.

Savings plan Scheme run by fund managers whereby investors purchase units on a regular basis.

Scheme particulars (UK) A document which provides full details of a unit trust and how it operates.

Scrip issue An issue of shares to existing shareholders in set proportion to their holdings in lieu of monetary dividend.

SEC (US) The Securities Exchange Commission is the federal agency that promotes full public disclosure and protects the investing public against malpractice in securities markets.

Securities and Investment Institute (UK) The professional body for qualified and experienced practitioners of good repute working in the securities and other financial services industry.

Share exchange scheme A scheme which enables investors to exchange equity holdings for shares or units in a fund.

SICAV (FR) Société d'Investissement à Capital Variable. French form of mutual fund.

Single pricing Pricing system where only one price is quoted, rather than separate buying and selling prices.

Sub-division of shares or units Shares or units are 'split' in a fixed ratio.

Switching discount Discount given when an investor switches from one fund to another.

Tax credit voucher Tax on income, whether distributed or re-invested, is paid automatically to the taxation authority and holders receive a 'voucher' in confirmation.

Total return A measure of performance which combines income and capital gain or loss.

Transfer agent (US) The organisation used by a mutual fund to maintain security records and handle share- or unitholder transactions.

Trust deed Legal document that contains basic details of the constitution of a fund that is a trust.

Trustee (UK) An institution which acts as custodian of a unit trust's assets on behalf of unitholders.

Umbrella funds (UK) A single authorised fund with any number of constituent parts or sub-funds.

Uncertificated See **Dematerialisation**.

Underwriting   Undertaking to support an issue of shares by agreeing to take up any that are unsubscribed, in exchange for a commission.

Unfranked income (UK)   Interest, commissions and dividends received from overseas companies – i.e., income that has been subject to UK corporation tax.

Unlisted Securities Market (USM) (UK)   The market, introduced by the UK Stock Exchange in 1980, open to companies which did not fulfil all the requirements of the Stock Exchange for a full quotation (*see also* **AIM**).

UCITS (EU)   Undertakings for Collective Investment in Transferable Securities. A European Union directive.

Warrants   Instrument entitling the holder to subscribe for another form of security on prescribed, usually favourable, terms.

Withholding tax   Tax deducted from dividends paid by foreign companies to non-residents.

Yield   Commonly, the percentage of the quoted offer price that represents the prospective annual income of the fund for its current annual accounting period, after deducting all charges, but see text for variations.

ABBREVIATIONS

....

ACD	Authorised Corporate Director
AGM	Annual General Meeting
AIM	Alternative Investment Market
ARROW	Advanced Risk Responsive Operating Framework
CAPM	Capital Asset Pricing Model
CD	Certificate of Deposit
CESR	Council of European Securities Regulators
CIF	Common Investment Fund
CONSOLS	Consolidated Stock
CP	Commercial Paper
CTF	Child Trust Fund
DIE	Designated Investment Exchange
DPB	Designated Professional Body
DTI	Department of Trade and Industry
EGM	Extraordinary General Meeting
EPS	Earnings Per Share
ER	Expected Return
FCP	Fond Commun de Placement
FSA	Financial Services Authority
FSAct	Financial Services Act 1986
FSMA	Financial Services & Markets Act
ICVC	Investment Company with Variable Capital
IMA	Investment Management Association
ISA	Individual Savings Accounts
ISD	Investment Services Directive
LME	London Metal Exchange
MRP	Market Risk Premium
NAV	Net Asset Value

NCIS	National Criminal Intelligence Service
OEIC	Open-Ended Investment Company
OFT	Office of Fair Trading
OPCVM	Organisme de Placement Collectif en Valeurs Mobilières
PE ratio	Price/Earnings ratio
PEG	Price/Earnings Growth ratio
PEP	Personal Equity Plan
PPE	Prospective Price/Earnings ratio
PRP	Portfolio Risk Premium
RCH	Recognised Clearing House
RIE	Recognised Investment Exchange
ROCE	Return On Capital Employed
SICAF	Société d'Investissement à Capital Fixe
SICAV	Société d'Investissement à Capital Variable
SLA	Service Levels Agreement
SML	Security Market Line
SRO	Self-Regulating Organisation
TPR	The Pensions Regulator
UCITS	Undertakings for Collective Investment in Transferable Securities
VCT	Venture Capital Trust
XD or xd	ex-distribution or ex-dividend

INDEX

Coventry University Library